DATE DUE

WITHDRAWN FROM
RCSJ LIBRARY

GENERALS VS. PRESIDENTS

Neomilitarism in Latin America

GENERALS VS. PRESIDENTS

Neomilitarism in Latin America

EDWIN LIEUWEN

PALL MALL PRESS

London

Published in Great Britain in 1964 by
The Pall Mall Press Ltd
77–79 Charlotte Street, London W. 1

Contents

1. Introduction   3

2. 1962: Two Down   10
   Argentina
   Peru

3. 1963: Four More to Go   37
   Guatemala
   Ecuador
   Dominican Republic
   Honduras

4. 1964: Brazil   69

5. Military Acquiescence in Social Reform   86
   Venezuela
   El Salvador

6. Military Intervention Today: A Comparative Analysis   95
   The Military Branch of Politics
   Military Involvement in the Social Revolution
   The Intervention Process
   The Seven Coups Compared
   The Consequences of Intervention

v

7. Kennedy and the Latin American Generals   114

    Encouragement of Democracy

    The Cuban Question

    Counterinsurgency

    A Policy Critique

8. Prospects   130

    Conservatism of the Contemporary Military Leaders

    Castro-Communism, Militarism, and Democracy

    Nasserism

9. Dilemma in Washington   142

    Johnson and the Latin American Generals

    Some Questions, Comments, and Suggestions

Bibliography   151

Index   155

GENERALS VS. PRESIDENTS

Neomilitarism in Latin America

1. Introduction

The hopes of the whole Western Hemisphere soared on March 13, 1961, when President John F. Kennedy proposed at a White House reception for Latin American diplomats an *"Alianza para el Progreso—*a vast cooperative effort, unparalleled in magnitude and nobility of purpose to satisfy the basic needs of the American people." As subsequently elaborated, this ambitious program calls for $20 billion in public and private investment in Latin America during the 1960's, with the over-all design being to eliminate hunger, to provide education for all, and to raise the living standards of every American family south of the Rio Grande.

An integral part of this bold new program of large-scale United States aid is a requirement that "political freedom must accompany material progress." "Our Alliance for Progress . . . must work to eliminate tyranny," said the President, and he added that the economic and political progress "must be accompanied by social change." The emphasis upon democratic progress sprang from a conviction that social change must come by peaceful evolution rather than violent revolution, and that political freedom could in itself break down the social barriers that had hitherto blocked change and reform in Latin America. Accordingly, the motto for the Alianza became *"Progreso sí, tiranía no."*

At the time the Alianza was proposed, there were good grounds for believing that the democratic, evolutionary path of social revolution might work. For rule by military men, traditionally the chief impediment to representative government and constitu-

3

tional processes, seemed to be ending. For example, in 1954, twelve of the twenty Latin American republics were ruled by generals or colonels who had originally achieved the presidency by the use of force, but by mid-1961, only one of these—General Alfredo Stroessner of Paraguay—remained. During this seven-year wave of antimilitarism, six of the military dictators were deposed by revolution (General Juan Perón in Argentina in 1955, Colonel Paul Magloire in Haiti in 1956, General Gustavo Rojas Pinilla in Colombia in 1957, General Marcos Pérez Jiménez in Venezuela in 1958, General Fulgencio Batista in Cuba in 1959, and Colonel José María Lemus in El Salvador in 1960); four were eliminated by assassination (Colonel José Antonio Remón in Panama in 1955, General Anastasio Somoza in Nicaragua in 1956, Colonel Carlos Castillo Armas in Guatemala in 1957, and General Rafael Trujillo in the Dominican Republic in 1961); while in Peru, the election of a civilian opposition candidate in 1956 brought an end to the dictatorial power of General Manuel Odría.

Small wonder, then, that optimism about the prospects for a democratic social revolution prevailed among the Western Hemisphere delegates who signed the Alliance for Progress Charter at Punta del Este, Uruguay, on August 17, 1961. The ambitious goals set forth in the charter included redistribution of the tax burden to bear more heavily on the wealthy; redistribution of agricultural holdings to the landless peasants; greatly improved health, housing, and education facilities; elimination of ruinous inflation; stabilization of export prices for commodities; integration of the Latin American economies; and encouragement of private enterprise. All these goals, of course, were aimed at rapidly raising the standard of living in order to alleviate Latin America's deepening social crisis.

Only eight months after the charter had been signed, however, the Argentine plans and programs ground to a virtual halt as a consequence of military intervention. The generals and admirals refused to accept the gains made by the Peronista Front in the congressional and gubernatorial elections of March 18, 1962.

Instead, they deposed President Arturo Frondizi and dismissed Congress, then squabbled among themselves for a year and a half over government policy before restoring constitutional government, in October, 1963.

Three months after the Argentine intervention, military leaders in Peru imposed a veto on democratic processes, again because the armed forces disapproved of the outcome of elections—those of June, 1962. They, too, deposed the President and Congress, then ruled through a junta for a full year until a President more acceptable to the armed forces was elected by the Peruvian people.

During 1963, four more constitutional governments were replaced through the use of physical force by military men. On March 30, 1963, a group of Army colonels in Guatemala arrested and exiled President Miguel Ydígoras Fuentes, suspended the constitution, dissolved the legislature, and proclaimed a ban on all political activity. Three months later, in Ecuador, the chiefs of the three armed services took similar action against the civilian political authorities. The contagion of military coups swept back to the Caribbean in September as President Juan Bosch and his democratic government in the Dominican Republic were ousted by the Army and Air Force. A similar blow at the hands of the military was suffered by the liberal government of President Villeda Morales of Honduras in early October of 1963.

Finally, Latin America's largest country, Brazil, came under military rule in early April of 1964. The officer corps removed President João Goulart for undermining military morale and "intending" to violate the constitution in an attempt to perpetuate himself in power.

All seven military coups deposed constitutional, duly elected Presidents.* All of them, with the possible exception of Peru, were counterrevolutionary movements, center-right actions against the labor-left.

Not only do the armed forces' chieftains retain power in all five

* Arosemena and Goulart had won popular elections to the Vice-Presidency prior to their constitutional succession to the Presidency.

nations where constitutional governments were destroyed during
1963 and 1964, but dictatorial regimes of some years' standing
continue to hold sway over Paraguay, Haiti, and Nicaragua. In
addition, further military coups could occur in Venezuela, El
Salvador, Chile, and Colombia.

Quite understandably, this resurgence of militarism in Latin
America was interpreted in Washington as a distinct setback for
the Alliance for Progress. Not only were the armed forces of Latin
America making a mockery of the democratic principles of the
Alianza, but they were also, by their intervention, stifling social
change. The danger was, now that the democratic avenue to social
revolution had been blocked in so many Latin American countries, that the desperate masses would increasingly be attracted to
Castro's Cuban way of violent social upheaval and Communism.
To a growing number in Latin America, especially the youth, the
Cuban experiment seemed to provide more hope of social justice
than the Alianza, which had been brought to a standstill by military coups in so many countries.

And what was the reaction in Washington? This book will try
to illuminate the profoundly significant changes made by President Kennedy in the traditional United States policy toward the
Latin American military. He attempted to make the democratic
hopes of the Alliance become reality by adopting a hard line toward governments coming to power through the use of force.
The Johnson Administration seems to have abandoned this
policy. In addition, Kennedy shifted the focus of United States
security policy in Latin America from the foreign threat to the
domestic one. The former emphasis upon collective action was
replaced by counterinsurgency and civic-action programs in individual countries. Even though he was not very successful in
achieving his objectives, the late President unquestionably demonstrated a new appreciation for, and adopted a fresh approach
toward, the difficult problems the United States Government
faced in dealing with Latin America's military leaders.

It is not the assumption of this book that the armed forces are the only impediment to achieving the Alliance for Progress goals, nor is it assumed that if the military stayed out of politics, all Latin America's social and economic problems would be resolved promptly. However, it is recognized that the armed forces are a key organization in relation to the socio-political crisis in most Latin American countries today. It is they who control the pace of social reform—either by giving civilians free rein, by threatening intervention against rapid reform, or by intervening either to bring it to a standstill or to conduct the reform process themselves. They are also the determining institution in relation to the practice of, or absence of, democracy. They can contribute much to making it work by protecting the duly elected civilian authorities against unconstitutional acts (as in Venezuela), they can water it down by forcibly transferring power from a government of the majority to one not truly representative (as in Argentina), or they can destroy it completely (as in the Dominican Republic).

It is not the intention of this book to rant against militarism. Rather, it is recognized that the intervention of the armed forces in Latin American politics is an objective fact of political life. Accordingly, the focus of this work is upon analysis and understanding of present-day militarism.

To this end, the emphasis is upon those seven countries that have recently experienced military coups (Argentina, Peru, Ecuador, Guatemala, the Dominican Republic, Honduras, and Brazil) and upon two more in which the military play rather unique roles (Venezuela and El Salvador). In all these nine countries, there is in process, or has recently been in process, a struggle between civilian and military rivals for political control, and in all of them a most serious social crisis exists. These countries contain over half of Latin America's population and land area and the bulk of its natural resources. Today all these countries are battlegrounds in the struggle between Communism and democracy in the Western Hemisphere.

Other Latin American countries also have problems with their military organizations, but elsewhere, except perhaps in Panama, the issue of civilian versus military control is neither so immediate nor so acute. In three countries, Nicaragua, Paraguay, and Haiti, the problem does not arise simply because the armed forces have long been politically dominant and civilian elements do not have the power potential to compete seriously with them. This may well again become the case in the Dominican Republic and Honduras, as well.

Conversely, in six other countries, military intervention is not a burning issue today simply because the armed forces there are not, at present, politically inclined institutions. In Uruguay, the last successful coup occurred back in the nineteenth century, in Mexico in 1920, and in Chile in 1925. Costa Rica destroyed her Army in 1948, and Bolivia followed suit in 1952; in both countries, the successor civilian regimes have been able thus far to control their new military organizations. Colombia's armed forces have traditionally remained aloof from politics, although they did assume power temporarily in 1953 to curb the threat of civil war.

The key assumption upon which my analysis of the problem of militarism rests is that an extremely acute social crisis exists in Latin America today, that the entire area is in the throes of a painful process of social, economic, and political transformation. Such an assumption is also the overriding theme noted by nearly every observer of the contemporary Latin American scene.

The symptoms of social revolution, already under way or imminent, are obvious. Half the people are undernourished and illiterate. The great majority are propertyless, for in most countries liquid and landed wealth is highly concentrated in the hands of very few. Most of the working population live and toil under conditions that retard health, welfare, and education. This situation is not new, but what is new are the desires, attitudes, and ambitions of the depressed masses. They have become spiritual soldiers of the "revolution of rising expectations." They are demanding prompt alleviation of their miseries, better opportunities, improved living standards, a greater share of their nation's wealth. Tremendous demographic pressures (a 3 per cent annual population growth) are adding daily to the force of these demands.

It is in this process of relentless social revolution that the armed forces of Latin America are so inexorably caught up today. If this book succeeds in shedding light upon the nature of, and the reasons for, their actions in relation to that social revolution, it will have achieved its major purpose.

One other purpose is to analyze the response and reaction of the United States to the phenomenon of neomilitarism in Latin America, particularly as it relates to the achievement, or lack of achievement, of the objectives of United States foreign policy.

2. 1962: Two Down

Argentina

On March 29, 1962, troops and tanks surrounded the Casa Rosada, the presidential palace, in downtown Buenos Aires. President Arturo Frondizi was arrested by officers of the armed forces. By nightfall he was a prisoner of the Argentine Navy on Martín García Island in the La Plata River. Thus ended a four-year experiment in constitutional government, and thus began again another of the military interregna that have punctuated Argentina's political history since 1930.

Why was Frondizi removed? The immediate cause was the March 18 elections—elections in which the *peronistas,* participating with their own candidates for the first time since the armed forces had ousted dictator Juan Perón in September, 1955, scored a smashing victory. The 2.5 million votes won by the Peronist Front represented 35 per cent of the total—more than any other party received. It spelled victory for *peronista* candidates for ten of the fourteen provincial governorships and for almost one-fourth of the seats in the Chamber of Deputies.

But these election results were unacceptable to the anti-*peronista* leadership of the armed forces. On March 19, the garrisons, ships, and air bases were alerted, and Army generals, Navy admirals, and Air Force brigadiers were summoned to their respective headquarters in the capital to deliberate on the election crisis. That same evening, President Frondizi issued orders for military interventors to assume power in those provinces where

10

the *peronistas* had won. Over the next ten days, military pressures upon the President to resign became overwhelming. When he refused to do so, he was removed by force.

President Frondizi, well aware that political normalcy and stability could never be restored to Argentina so long as the powerful labor-leftist vote was suppressed by force and legal restrictions, hoped to woo the *peronista* element—which had cast nearly 1 million blank protest votes in the 1960 elections—back into the body politic. He apparently believed that the *peronistas* had begun to forget their erstwhile leader (by then more than six years in exile) and that the reasonable policies of his government were such that the labor-left would forsake the *peronista* candidates and add to the strength of his own ruling Intransigent Radical Civic Union (Unión Cívica Radical Intransigente, or UCRI) party. Convinced himself, he somehow convinced the military hierarchy that the time was ripe for the UCRI and the Popular Radical Civic Union (Unión Cívica Radical Popular, or UCRP), both moderate, middle-class parties, to capture most of the old *peronista* vote. Instead, both were routed in the March 18 debacle.

This gross error in political judgment was but the immediate reason for Frondizi's fall, for the military had been restless under his rule from the day he took office in 1958. During the 1955–58 military interregnum, Provisional President General Pedro Aramburu and his Army-Navy-Air Force junta had sought energetically to "de-Peronize" the nation in preparation for restoring the government to responsible civilian leadership. Accordingly, Peronism was variously described by the military hierarchy as an obscurantist tyranny utterly alien to the Argentine national tradition, an irresponsible totalitarian philosophy that had morally corrupted the nation's youth and its politicians, a socio-political system that was leading the nation directly down the path of social dissolution and Communism. Although armed-forces officers wrangled over how long it should take to "de-Peronize" and how hard the anti-*peronista* line should be, and although there was constant jockey-

ing for power, the Aramburu government demonstrated a remarkable capacity to survive repeated crises. During 1958,
Aramburu managed to hold elections, in which the *peronista*
party was outlawed and its candidates barred. The triumphant
candidate was Frondizi, with his left-of-center UCRI party.

The Frondizi-UCRI victory, however, was not the outcome the
military leadership had hoped to achieve. Their choice was the
centrist UCRP party, headed by Ricardo Balbín. Moreover, Frondizi was suspect for having won by questionable means—to wit,
his close adviser Rogelio Frigerio had called on Perón in Ciudad
Trujillo during the campaign, and the subsequent *peronista* vote
for Frondizi thus smacked of a deal. Its terms, as subsequently
publicized, included *peronista* control of organized labor, legalization of their party, and the eventual return to Argentina of Perón
himself.

As a consequence of the manner in which he had achieved
victory, Frondizi, from the very beginning, had to engage in a
kind of balancing act between the armed forces and the *peronistas*.
He had to coddle the labor-left if he ever hoped to strengthen his
fragile regime. Yet, if he moved too far in that direction, he
would provoke a military coup.

Although the armed forces frequently charged the President
with leading the nation down the road to Communism, his economic policies and his economic advisers, notably Alvaro Alsogaray, were unquestionably capitalistic. Foreign investors were
encouraged to help develop Argentina, and an austerity program
was launched that penalized the labor-left more heavily than any
other social group. Moreover, Washington apparently approved of
Frondizi's policies, for it lent him emergency financial assistance
and indicated its intention to support his economic and social-reform plans under the Alliance for Progress program.

Frondizi's problem with the armed forces, then, was essentially
political, but the political problem was charged with the dynamite
of social change. Thus, the Argentine political drama in the years
1958–62 revealed a wobbly President attempting to maintain his

balance between the labor-left and the military. In an effort to survive, he alternated favors. He allowed *peronistas* to control the trade unions and promised them political rights, while, on the other hand, he used the armed forces to control striking workers and supported military demands for substantial pay raises and liberal purchases of equipment. Until his suicidal decision to legalize *peronista* participation in the elections of March 18, 1962, Frondizi's tightrope act was amazingly successful.

Military pressures upon the President were by no means uniform. In fact, there were complicated splits among the services that must be traced from their origins in order to understand the 1963 denouement of the civilian-military crisis and to appreciate the problems Argentina has yet to face in this sphere.

In the Army, following Perón's overthrow, in 1955, three main currents of political thought emerged. General Eduardo Lonardi, who ruled the country for four months, represented those who wanted to take a moderate line toward *peronista* officers and to reintegrate the labor-left back into the political system as soon as possible. But Lonardi was soon ousted by the Aramburu faction, which demanded a thoroughgoing purge of the *peronistas,* both military and civilian. Another factor in Lonardi's downfall was the opposition of Masons in Aramburu's group to the strong Catholic element around him.

With the end of the Lonardi government, officers with labor-leftist sympathies were driven underground. The leader of this faction was Colonel Manuel Raimundes, who formed the secret Green Dragon Lodge. Through it, he attempted to acquaint young Army officers with Argentina's social problems and to convince them they had a special political and social responsibility toward the labor-left. Under the Aramburu government, Raimundes carried on his intrigues by correspondence from his post as a military attaché in London. Under Frondizi, he attempted to win converts from the vantage point of his newly acquired position in the War Ministry. In this activity, he was opposed by the anti-*peronista* officers. The upshot of this struggle was the dismissal in 1959 of Raimundes and the Green Dragon officers.

But even before the purge of the suspected *peronistas* was complete, a division occurred among the anti-*peronistas*. There emerged during the Aramburu Administration (1955–58) a group of hard-line officers who wanted to rule the nation indefinitely, or at least until such time as the political system of Argentina was thoroughly rid of the *peronista* virus. This group became known as the *"gorilas,"* and its strength centered in the infantry and engineering branches of the Army. The engineers, under General Pío Martejena, had their special secret Hammer and Piston Lodge.

Aramburu was able to control the *gorilas,* but following the inauguration of Frondizi, they whittled away the President's strength until they achieved his overthrow in March, 1962. For example, during 1959–60, in addition to purging the Army of Green Dragon officers, the *gorilas* pursued and prosecuted civilian *peronistas* without presidential authorization or support. Also, they forced the resignation of two insufficiently anti-*peronista* War Ministers. During 1961, the President removed *gorila* leader General Carlos Toranzo Montero as Commander in Chief of the Army, but his post was quickly assumed by General Raúl A. Poggi, a fellow *gorila,* who then took the lead in ousting the President.

In the wake of Aramburu's retirement in 1958, there emerged still a third Army group, which adopted an intermediate line between the *gorilas* and the Green Dragons. These moderates had their principal strength in the cavalry, which commanded the motorized units, including all the tanks, and the strategic Campo de Mayo garrison just outside Buenos Aires. They believed that the government should be restored to civilian authorities but that the *peronistas* should be restricted for an indefinite period by electoral controls. It is this moderate group that is dominant in the Army today. Its leader, and now the most powerful soldier in Argentina, is General Juan Onganía, commander of the all-important cavalry branch of the Army.

In contrast to the Army, the Navy remained unified throughout the 1955–63 period of political crisis. Its position was unmistakably clear and unwavering. From the time of the 1943 revolution, it has been unalterably opposed to Perón. The Navy officer corps (unlike the Army's, which is petty-bourgeois in class origin) tends to originate in the upper-middle class, a class traditionally opposed to any socio-political advance of the labor-left. What is more, the Navy's democratic traditions, albeit of the classical Greek, privileged-class type, conflicted with Perón's proletarian-oriented authoritarianism. It took Perón nearly a full year, for example, to find a high-ranking officer willing to head the Navy Ministry. The Navy participated in an abortive plot to oust Perón in February of 1944 and in a temporarily successful one in October of 1945. Following Perón's triumphant return and consolidation of power in the period 1945–55, the Navy continued to resist all Perón's gestures of cooperation and to work toward his downfall. Perón, in retaliation, lavished funds upon the Army and Air Force while drastically curtailing the Navy's budget and denying it any new combat equipment.

Following Perón's downfall, the Navy made a political and material comeback. It advertised itself as "the only service uncorrupted by Peronism" and claimed chief credit for ridding the nation of the tyrant. The Navy's unified, hard-line position with respect to "de-Peronization" gave it a strength out of all proportion to its numbers. The Army had 80,000 men, the Navy less than 20,000, yet on the five-man junta that ruled Argentina from 1955 to 1958, the Navy had two men, led by Vice-President Isaac Rojas, the Army had two, and the Air Force one. Other elements of Navy strength included the Buenos Aires police, over which it gained control following the 1955 revolution, and the Infantería de Marina (Marine Corps). The latter, only 2,000 strong in 1955, had increased to nearly 8,000 by 1963.

In addition, the Navy began to recover the ground lost during the lean Perón years by demanding, and usually getting, special funds for equipment. In 1956, it acquired an aircraft carrier and soon thereafter, despite opposition from the Air Force, a naval air arm. During 1961 alone, it purchased three new destroyers, expanded and modernized its bases, and exacted from Congress (in secret session) an accord for a $265-million ship and aircraft purchasing program.*

The Navy's political power was demonstrated by its key role not only in defeating Perón, but also in bringing down the Lonardi government four months later and Frondizi in March of 1962. Since 1955, the Navy line has always been uncompromisingly anti-*peronista*. The Navy agreed only conditionally to support Aramburu's drive to restore civilian political control, but when Frondizi won the 1958 elections, the Navy soon gravitated toward the *gorila* position. It, too, advocated military rule until such time as the nation fully recovered from the moral sickness and social destruction wrought by Perón.

The Air Force, the newest of the services, was not so deeply involved politically as the Army and the Navy. Also, being weaker than the other two, the Air Force tended to be cautious in each interservice struggle and not to take sides until its resolution was near. However, the power of the Air Force, particularly the firepower of its jets and bombers, has nearly always been sufficient to swing the balance between the contending Army and Navy factions. In order to play this kind of opportunistic political game, the Air Force brigadiers have frequently found it necessary to sacrifice their service secretary, and even their commander in chief, but they have considered this a small price to pay for the enviable advantage of always being on the winning side.

The Air Force was built up mainly by Perón. However, as military resistance to the dictator grew, rebel plotters found ready Air Force defectors. In the June, 1955, uprising, the Air Force bombed the Casa Rosada, and in the September, 1955, revolt, it played a key role in bringing the dictatorship to an end.

The Air Force's record for picking the winners has been im-

* Rogelio García Lupo, *La rebelión de los generales* (Buenos Aires: Proceso, 1962), pp. 39-45.

peccable. It backed Aramburu against Lonardi, and under Aramburu, it fought both the Green Dragons and the *gorilas*. In March of 1962, it backed the *gorilas* and the Navy in bringing down Frondizi, then switched to the "moderates" to help defeat the *gorilas* in September of 1962 and the Navy in April of 1963.

Before recounting the great politico-military drama that shook the Argentine nation in the period from March, 1962, to April, 1963, it is necessary to say something of the military decision-making process. As soon as a serious political issue develops, the Navy, Air, and War Secretaries summon their commanders to the capital. In the Navy Building, a *junta de almirantes* (council of admirals), consisting of all nineteen admirals, meets in a closed conference room. The issue is placed before the group; the junior admiral states his position first, followed by the next in rank on up to the Chief of Naval Operations; a consensus is arrived at; the entire group agrees to support this position. A similar process, consisting of a like number of brigadiers sitting in conference, determines the Air Force position, which is usually to stand aloof until the last possible moment. More complicated is the Army decision-making process, for here the number involved is about a hundred, and the splits are so deep that a consensus is very difficult to arrive at. Even though the engineers and infantry come up with a majority vote, for example, the cavalry does not consider this a mandate for supporting a unified Army position. More often than not, the minority pursues a line of independent action.

Although united in their moves to oust Frondizi, the armed forces were by no means in agreement as to what to do next. Effective power, for a very brief period in late March, 1962, resided in the three service heads (Army Commander in Chief General Raúl A. Poggi, Chief of Naval Operations Admiral Augustín A. Penas, and Air Force Commander in Chief Brigadier Cayo Antonio Alsina), rather than in the service secretaries. Poggi, Penas, and Alsina, all of them notorious hard-liners with respect to the *peronistas* and civilian control, constituted themselves into a junta and apparently were prepared to rule Argentina. Poggi himself cleared the Casa Rosada and appeared to have had ideas about assuming the provisional presidency. However, soon after Frondizi's arrest, Senate President José María Guido, constitutional successor to the presidency, went before the Supreme Court and was sworn in.*

President Guido, a UCRI politician, was then in a curious position. He was under pressure from all the leading political parties (the Peronista Front, UCRI, and UCRP) to honor the March 18 elections and seat the *peronista* governors and congressmen, while the service heads demanded annulment of the elections. But the service heads did not speak for all the officers. The cavalrymen let Guido know they had little faith in either Poggi or War Secretary General Mariano Bartolomé Carreras, both of whom were infantry officers. The President also became aware of a serious Air Force split between Secretary Brigadier Jorge Rojas Silveyra, who took a moderate position on the *peronista* problem, and Alsina.

On April 20, Guido made his move. He dismissed Carreras and appointed as War Secretary Enrique Rauch, a cavalry general and commander of Campo de Mayo. To stop Rauch from taking over Army Headquarters, Poggi deployed troops at strategic positions around the government buildings and in downtown Buenos Aires. Unimpressed, Rauch left Campo de Mayo, leading a tank battalion toward the center of the city. Just as the infantry and cavalry were about to engage in battle, Guido arranged a compromise. Both Rauch and Poggi agreed to give up their posts, and their positions, War Secretary and Commander in Chief of the Army, were assumed, temporarily, by General Juan Bautista Loza, a former infantryman but not a hard-line *gorila*.

Thereupon the officers and the President worked out a compromise on the *peronista* and civilian-rule problems. The March 18 elections were declared null and void. Congress was declared in recess, and new elections for both President and Congress were

* Guido's action infuriated Poggi, who reportedly went so far as to threaten Guido with a revolver in a futile attempt to make him resign.

scheduled for 1963. Since this decision made none of the political parties happy, Guido soon found himself governing without any organized civilian support. After May of 1962, he was little more than a puppet of the military, buffeted about the stage at will by the Navy and by the competing cliques in the Army and the Air Force.

The decision to hold elections, which the Navy, part of the Air Force, and the *gorila* group in the Army opposed, did not clarify the future political role of the *peronistas*. Throughout July, the military and their legal advisers debated various formulas. It was tentatively agreed that a proportional system of representation must replace the old Sáenz Peña law, under which a majority vote in a province gave a party two-thirds of the representation, and that the *peronistas* must be prohibited from establishing their own party and putting up their own candidates.

But this formula was much too mild for the *gorilas*. They wanted no elections at all. The Rauch-Poggi crisis in April had merely tabled the outstanding problem between the moderates (now called *"legalistas"*) and the *gorilas,* and the latter now decided to resolve it. On August 8, General Federico Toranzo Montero, Commander of the Fourth Army Corps at Salta in northwest Argentina and brother of former *gorila* chief Carlos Toranzo Montero, demanded the resignation of Army Commander-War Secretary Loza, whom he considered a compromiser on the *peronista* issue. He called on all interior commands for support. The Navy backed him; the Air Force remained aloof. On August 9, all Army generals assembled at the War Ministry, but the differences between the *legalista* cavalry forces and the *gorila* infantry-engineer forces could be neither resolved nor compromised at the conference table.

On August 10, Guido dismissed Loza and tried another neutral candidate, General Eduardo Señorans, but the *gorilas,* now ready to fight for their position, refused to allow Señorans to enter the War Ministry. Thereupon, the cavalry prepared for battle. The tanks at Campo de Mayo, fifteen miles northwest of Buenos Aires, and at Magdalena, eighty miles to the southeast, were ordered to advance on the capital. Toranzo Montero, meanwhile, set up headquarters at the War Ministry. He ordered the capital's infantry garrison, the Buenos Aires police, and the Marine Corps to block the streets and blow up bridges, if necessary, to keep the tanks out. As the Air Force remained on the fence, this maneuver was successful, and the *gorilas* got the upper hand. Their partisans were appointed to the War Ministry and Army Commander posts. On September 6, they forced Guido to dissolve Congress, which had merely been in recess, and began pressuring him to call off the 1963 elections.

But the *legalista* cavalry was still to be heard from. The *gorila* chief had transferred the commander of Campo de Mayo, General Luis Caro, to an innocuous desk post in the War Ministry and announced the retirement of cavalry commander General Juan Onganía. The latter's response, on September 18, was to order an assault by the Campo de Mayo and Magdalena tank battalions upon the infantry entrenched in Buenos Aires. By September 20, the tanks were on the outskirts of the city, and the Air Force refused to defend the *gorilas*. Guido, at this juncture, dismissed the *gorila* Army heads, including Toranzo, whereupon the Navy declared itself in rebellion against the government. The Air Force countered by grounding all Army transport planes, thus preventing troops from the interior from reinforcing the capital, and strafed several *gorila* positions inside the capital. Meanwhile, tanks overcame several *gorila* antiaircraft batteries. The issue was resolved in favor of the cavalrymen on the night of September 23, before the Navy ships could arrive to shell Buenos Aires.

Thus the *legalistas* triumphed, and now the purge of the *gorilas* began. The new Army Commander, General Onganía, ordered the arrest and imprisonment of nearly 200 *gorila* officers, replaced them all with *legalistas,* dismissed four leading admirals, and wrested control of the capital police from the Navy.

Only the Air Force, which had again picked the winner, escaped the purge. There was, however, a problem concerning its Commander in Chief, Alsina. He had been a political chameleon ever since Frondizi's ouster. He had supported whichever Army faction had the upper hand at any given moment, and when the Navy had definitely lost out in the September crisis, he even advocated bombarding it. A majority of the brigadiers, restless under his leadership, called on Guido early in December and demanded Alsina's ouster. The President complied, whereupon Alsina, from the Córdoba Air Force Base, announced himself in rebellion. The Army gave Alsina no backing, and the Navy was in no mood to support the man who had so recently threatened them. Air Force jets from other bases kept the Córdoba planes on the ground while cadets and junior Air Force officers overwhelmed Alsina and the base command, thus nipping this rebellion in the bud.

Air Force Secretary Eduardo McLaughlin thereupon made it known publicly that his service was unequivocally supporting the scheduled mid-1963 elections, albeit with safeguards to prevent the *peronistas* from running their own candidates or having their own party. This stand, of course, coincided precisely with the position of the now dominant *legalista* group in the Army.

However, this position was unacceptable to the battered, but still not thoroughly beaten, Navy. It still wanted no elections at all. What the Navy feared was another covert alliance between the *peronistas* and the UCRI, whereupon the country would revert to the Frondizi-type political system of the 1958–62 period.

On April 2, 1963, the Navy announced it was rebelling against "Guido's fraudulent and undemocratic government, which was undermining the nation's institutions." How could it hope to win? Apparently it was counting on Army and Air Force defection, for recently retired officers of these two services, including Toranzo Montero and Alsina, were among the rebels. But as the expected Army and Air Force defections did not occur, the fighting was confined to the coastal area. Navy planes attempted to knock out the Magdalena tank base, and the Marines attempted to seize strategic positions in the capital. Both failed. Instead, tanks and loyal troops began assaulting the naval bases at Indio, Río Santi-

ago, and Puerto Belgrano, while the Air Force destroyed part of
the Navy's air arm on the ground and the rest flew to safety in
Uruguay. By April 5, it was all over. The Navy had taken a
severe beating. Its once proud Marine Corps, hated by the Army,
was ordered reduced by more than two-thirds (from 8,000 to
2,500), its air arm, hated by the Air Force, had been virtually
eliminated, and its powerful political voice was muted as its remaining fifteen admirals were retired and replaced by juniors of
a less recalcitrant stripe.

With the political issue inside the armed forces resolved, the
elections went forward on schedule. To prevent another UCRI-
peronista tie-up, the military forced Guido to take precautionary
measures. During May, he outlawed the Popular Union, a mere
screen party of the *peronistas,* and during June, the government
engaged in sufficient political persecution to bring about the
collapse of another UCRI-*peronista* front. On July 7, election
day, the outcome so fervently desired by the dominant *legalista*
element of the armed forces was obtained: The centrist UCRP
now triumphed. It won the presidency, control of the Senate, and
the largest number of seats in the House, with 26 per cent of the
total vote. On October 12, 1963, the armed forces transferred
power to Dr. Arturo Illía and his party, and retired to their barracks once more.

Argentina by the fall of 1964 was no closer to reintegrating the
labor-left into the political system than it was nine years previous,
when Perón fell. By 1955, labor-leftist forces had for almost a
decade controlled not only the presidency but both houses of
Congress as well. Since then, they have had no direct political representation whatsoever. In the 1960 congressional elections, with
their party outlawed, they cast, in protest, nearly 1 million blank
ballots. When legalized, in the March, 1962, elections, they
emerged as the strongest party, only to see their gains nullified by
force of arms. Once more outlawed, in the July, 1963, elections,
they again cast protest blank votes; their 18 per cent of the total
vote was exceeded only by the winning UCRP party.

The *peronista* vote is still virtually synonymous with that of the labor-left. Most military men will vehemently deny that their opposition to Peronism has anything to do with social antagonism toward the masses. In the case of the Navy, however, given the upper-middle-class origins of its officers, its position can largely be explained as a determination to keep the lower-income groups from exercising political influence. Peronism is merely a convenient label used to block all political and social change. Navy spokesmen frequently equated Peronism and Communism, and charged Frondizi with fostering both.

In the case of the Army officers, antipathies toward the *peronistas* are more genuinely personal. On social grounds, such antipathies make no sense at all, for most Army cadets have lower-middle-class origins. What is more, the great bulk of today's Army officer corps was closely associated with Perón in his heyday. In fact, Army cadets were often selected by the *peronista* party, and labor and the Army cooperated in defending the dictator against the center and the right. It is precisely because they are tainted with a *peronista* past that present-day Army leaders are so uncompromising in their anti-Peronism. For once having defected, they must ever reckon with the possibility of *peronista* vengeance. Thus the political actions of the Army officers today are largely motivated by a determination to save their own skins.

The anti-Peronism of the Air Force officers appears to be a complex mixture of individual hatreds and fears joined with the social conservatism of their service.*

Is it possible to keep a major segment of the socio-economic system, that is, the labor-left, politically emasculated for an extended period of time by use of force? A reading of recent Argentine history suggests that it might be. In the 1930 revolution, the middle classes, which had controlled Argentina politi-

---

* During 1961, U.S. Ambassador Roy R. Rubottom was forced out of his post, reportedly by the Air Force brigadiers, who had learned that he had expressed a lack of confidence in their service and had, accordingly, opposed their requests to the Pentagon for new jets.

cally for fourteen years, were ousted by upper social groups, which, in conjunction with the armed forces, held power for thirteen years until Perón triumphed. Today, it is the middle-class parties, the UCRI and the UCRP, that are keeping the labor-left down by legal devices and the use of force. They are by no means comfortable in this role, but the military, as Frondizi found out, leave them no choice.

After a number of years—it will probably take another decade, at least—the personalist associations of Peronism will certainly begin to die down, and the labor-left may then be able to partici-pate again politically. The Army is the service most likely to con-done, perhaps even to encourage, this. That the Army is the most socially conscious of the three services is apparent from its *peronista* heritage and from the activity of such lodges as the Green Dragons. Today there is much talk of Nasserism, the military-dominated political system of contemporary Egypt. This reflects the Army's social conscience at work, its feeling that it still has a revolutionary mission to fulfill, a duty to promote social change and reform in Argentina. A leading *nasserista* is said to be General Carlos Rosas. He had command of an Army corps, lost it when the *gorilas* triumphed in August of 1962, regained it when the *legalistas* recovered power in September. Rosas reportedly has many followers among the young officers, but the inevitable con-fusion between Nasserism and Peronism will probably render the *nasseristas* relatively powerless for some time.

When recent Argentine socio-political history is recounted, a rather somber panorama emerges. Here was a nation that prior to 1930 experienced nearly a half-century of civilian dominance. During this time, its economy prospered, its people became well-fed, and during the 1920's, the leaders of its rapidly growing middle class developed a workable system of responsible, rep-resentative government.

However, since 1930, the society, the economy, and the political structure have broken down badly. The upper-income groups, the middle classes, and the labor-left have been at war with one another. No government representing a workable consensus has been able to emerge. The three main classes themselves have frequently further divided into feuding factions. For example, if the middle-class UCRI and UCRP parties had cooperated on a slate of candidates in the March, 1962, elections, they would have received 50 per cent of the vote and thus defeated the *peronistas*.

Into this socio-political crisis, the armed forces have increasingly entered as regulators and moderators, sometimes of their own volition, sometimes at the urging of beleaguered civilian politicians. Once involved, the military have been unable to extricate themselves, and thus Argentina's political history since 1930 has been one of power alternating between military juntas and civilian regimes so feeble they must be shored up by military force in order to survive.

What is so perplexing about the Argentine case is that all the preconditions for a stable civilian democratic political system and for orderly evolutionary social change seem to be present. For here is the most economically and culturally advanced nation in all Latin America. Yet when one ponders its sour contemporary socio-political system, the apprehension arises that its sad destiny may await other Latin American states as they progress economically and culturally to the Argentine level. The basic ingredients are certainly present elsewhere—the compartmentalized societies, the uncompromising political factions, and the powerful, politically inclined military organizations, which serve as arbiters in the area's seemingly irreconcilable social and political crisis.

Peru

In the early morning hours of July 18, 1962, 200 antiguerrilla commandos, clad in full jungle-warfare regalia, arrived at the presidential palace in Lima and demanded admission. When this was refused, the Second Armored Division, backing up the commandos, sent one of its Sherman tanks crashing through the gates. President Manuel Prado was arrested and imprisoned on a Navy ship, Congress was dismissed, and a four-man military junta, consisting of the Chairman of the Joint Chiefs of Staff and the Commanders of the Army, Navy, and the Air Force, assumed control of the government of Peru. The June 10, 1962, presidential and congressional elections were declared null and void.

The armed forces had intervened, explained junta President General Manuel Pérez Godoy, in order to "preserve democracy." Junta spokesmen explained that although there had been unmistakable evidence of electoral fraud, the National Electoral Board, constitutionally empowered to rule on such matters, had chosen to play politics and ignore the evidence. In addition, they explained, President Prado had attempted to intervene in the election crisis in a manner that tended to distort the will of the Peruvian people. The military leaders charged that such actions by irresponsible civilian authorities were intolerable, and so they had intervened, as generals had done repeatedly throughout Peru's history, in order to save their country.

It is true that the June 10 elections had produced some most unusual results. Seven parties campaigned, but basically there was a three-cornered struggle among Fernando Belaúnde Terry of the Popular Action Party (Acción Popular, or AP), Víctor Raúl Haya de la Torre of the American Revolutionary Popular Alliance (Alianza Popular Revolucionaria Americana, or APRA), and former President General Manuel Odría of the Odriísta National Union (Unión Nacional Odriísta, or UNO). The race was extremely close. Haya de la Torre emerged with a 15,000-vote plurality, his vote representing just under 33 per cent of the total. Belaúnde had 32 per cent, and Odría 28 per cent. The constitution states that election to the presidency requires that the candidate receive at least one-third of the votes cast. Since none met this requirement, Congress was empowered to select a President from among the three leading contenders. In the new Congress, APRA, with 45 per cent of the membership, was easily the dominant party, and quite understandably, it expected to make an alliance with either the AP or the UNO to elect Haya de la Torre.

While this congressional maneuvering was going on, however, military leaders informed Haya de la Torre on July 3 that he was not acceptable to them. Thereupon, he publicly withdrew his candidacy. APRA then began discussing possible alliances with AP and UNO leaders. After these talks, APRA decided to support Odría in exchange for a powerful role in his government. But this arrangement was also unacceptable to the military leadership, and to forestall its execution, they seized the government and annulled the elections. Apparently, Belaúnde was the only candidate acceptable to the armed forces, and since he had been unable to win within established legal and constitutional procedures, he welcomed the military takeover.

Was there any truth to the charge of electoral fraud? Prior to the elections, armed-forces leaders had warned against the possibility of irregularities, and to prevent them, they required a military identification card of all voters and imported a special indelible finger ink to prevent multiple voting. The Army supervised the elections. As the early returns favored AP, zone commanders were quick to announce Belaúnde the victor. When later returns showed Haya de la Torre forging into the lead, the military leaders asserted that, despite its diligent efforts, fraud had been committed in seven northern departments where APRA ran up large majorities. The Army's evidence of fraud was presented to the National Electoral Board (where both AP and APRA were represented), but it was rejected as inconclusive. When the junta seized power, it promised to produce evidence of widespread fraud, but despite periodic requests by the press that it do so, it was either unable or unwilling to comply.

Quite obviously, the fraud charge was merely the cloak used by the military to mask their implacable hostility toward Haya and his party. To understand this attitude, it is necessary to go back about thirty years into Peruvian history. Until the Great Depression, Peruvian politics had been pretty much the exclusive preserve of the military and the oligarchy. The latter is a landed and commercial elite, then, as now, consisting of less than 2 per cent of the population. The rest of Peru's society, the small middle class and a great mass of illiterate, poverty-stricken Indians and mestizos, counted for almost nothing politically.

In manning the governmental machinery, officers of the armed forces traditionally played a leading role. When they triumphed over the Spanish forces in 1824, Bolívar informed them that "your fatherland will always reckon you among the first saviors of Peru," and they considered themselves saviors ever after. Their deep and constant involvement in the nation's politics gave them a great sense of self-importance, a feeling of natural superiority over civilian politicians.

In protest against the traditional military-oligarchic rule, a nationalistic reform movement, APRA, was organized during the 1920's. This party demanded social and political integration of the Indian masses, redistribution of the nation's wealth, and nationalization of foreign holdings. It also advocated removal of military men from politics. It claimed that it was not the enemy of the armed forces, but that it merely wanted to convert them into a modern professional organization exclusively devoted to the military functions of defending against possible foreign aggression and preserving internal order. APRA stood for constitutionalism and the rule of law under civilian authorities.

In the elections of 1931, the military candidate, Colonel Luis Sánchez Cerro, was pitted against Haya de la Torre. Following a campaign in which the troops and *apristas* engaged in sporadic skirmishes, Sánchez Cerro was declared the winner in an obviously rigged election. In protest, frustrated *apristas* assaulted an Army garrison in Trujillo, massacring both officers and men. In retaliation, soldiers slaughtered hundreds of *apristas*.

Ever since, there has been no peace between APRA and the military. Sánchez Cerro was assassinated in 1933—"by *apristas*," according to the military. General Oscar Benavides and oligarch Manuel Prado ran Peru between 1933 and 1945, during which

time APRA was outlawed as a party and its leaders were persecuted. Newly legalized in 1945, the party made a comeback, winning control of Congress under the middle-of-the-road Administration of José Luis Bustamante (1945–48). But the armed forces
never really accepted the *apristas*. Interior Minister General
Manuel Odría repeatedly accused them of fomenting strikes and
inciting violence. When the legislative machinery came to a
standstill in 1948 as a result of the refusal of conservative Congressmen to attend so that a quorum could be formed, both
APRA and the military conspired to gain control. As the Army
prepared a coup against Bustamante, APRA countered by in-
stigating a mutiny of the petty officers in the Navy. On October
27, 1948, General Odría seized the government, outlawed APRA,
and set up a military dictatorship that lasted for eight years. For
more than five of these years, Haya de la Torre was a virtual
prisoner in asylum inside the Colombian Embassy in Lima.

In the 1956 elections, APRA cooperated with the oligarch
Manuel Prado and his Peruvian Democratic Party against Belaúnde and against Odría's candidate, in exchange for promises of
early legalization of their party. During Prado's Administration,
APRA attempted to avoid all controversy with the armed forces
and to gain military acceptance of their increasingly moderate,
nonviolent political movement.

The heritage of the past, however, was too strong. Army officers
could neither forgive nor forget. The history of APRA's long
hostility toward this institution had become an integral part of
every cadet's education, and the Army had observed the anniversary of the Trujillo massacres in solemn ceremony each year
since 1932. During the 1962 campaign, military leaders frequently
issued subtle warnings that they might not accept the popular will
in the presidential elections if it turned out contrary to their institution's interests. The voters, the National Electoral Council,
and President Prado had each in turn ignored these warnings.*

* On June 17, President Prado tried to pave the way for military acceptance of
Haya by ordering the transfer of the notoriously anti-Haya Air Force Chief,

This left the military no other way to block Haya de la Torre and APRA except by use of force.

What did the military coup mean? Quite obviously, it meant the veto of Haya de la Torre and APRA. What else did it mean? Was this another case of the soldiers intervening on behalf of the oligarchs to stifle social change and reform? This interpretation at first seemed plausible as business and landholding groups and the Church hierarchy openly condoned the military's action. Adding fuel to this view was Washington's stern protest against the coup and its public lament that this was a severe setback for the reform aims of the Alliance for Progress.

However, the rightist-reaction thesis left some unanswered questions. Why did Prado and at least part of the oligarchy support Haya de la Torre? Why did the military also apparently refuse to accept Odría, a former military man and certainly the most conservative of the candidates?

Some of the confusion with respect to the role and motives of the armed-forces leadership began to clear up once the junta assumed power. Although General Pérez Godoy, as senior officer, assumed the ceremonial duties of President, the other three members of the military junta, War Minister General Nicolás Lindley López, Air Minister General Pedro Vargas Prada, and Navy Minister Vice-Admiral Francisco Torres Matos, also assumed the title of President. Within a few days after taking power, the junta had released all political prisoners,* restored civil rights, and promised to hold new elections in June of 1963. In these elections, the public was assured, no member of the junta would be a candidate. A nonpartisan election committee was appointed to draft a new electoral law.

As expected, there was trouble from APRA. Still nominally in control of most of organized labor, the party called a general strike

---

General Pedro Vargas Prada, to the Inter-American Defense Board in Washington. However, when forty top Air Force officers resigned in protest, Prado had to withdraw his order.

* Prado went into exile in Paris.

in protest against the military takeover, but only 10 per cent of the workers responded. The junta, thereupon, throughout the remainder of the year, attempted to destroy the *aprista* trade-union leadership by favoring competing Communist leaders whenever control of a union was contested.*

However, the junta very soon demonstrated it was no lackey of the oligarchy. During its very first month in power, it issued decrees fixing minimum wages and salaries and assessing stiff fines (a hitherto unheard-of penalty) for tax evasion. On November 16, after three months of study and discussion with experts, the junta issued an interim agrarian-reform decree that empowered the state to expropriate unproductive lands and to redistribute them to the Indian peasantry.

In their administrative and reform efforts, the four uniformed presidents appeared to have the solid backing of all three armed services. Dissension within the junta did become evident in early 1963, but this was a problem of personalities rather than issues. Pérez Godoy apparently began to develop ambitions and attempted to assume the authority, as well as the routine and ceremonial duties, of President. He began making television addresses without consulting the other three Presidents. To his colleagues, these "personalistic" policies were intolerable, and so General Pérez Godoy was removed on March 3, and General Lindley became Acting President.

Soon thereafter, the military rulers, true to their promises, decreed an improved electoral law (which placed the controversial National Electoral Council under the judiciary rather than under the executive) and provided a free and open atmosphere in which

---

* This maneuver backfired, however, for the Communist leadership, toward the end of the year, encouraged land seizures in the interior, promoted strikes on the sugar plantations and docks on the coast, and became involved in wanton destruction in the Cerro de Pasco mining complex in the Andes. In early January, 1963, the junta reacted by arresting nearly 3,000 leaders in connection with an alleged "red plot" to assassinate the Army leadership and seize control of the government. Ironically, APRA applauded the junta for its action.

the parties could campaign for the scheduled June, 1963, presidential and congressional elections.

The 1963 campaign was a carbon copy of that of 1962. Belaúnde, Haya de la Torre, and Odría were again the principal candidates. The same parties participated, the same platforms were announced, and the issues were the same as in 1962—with one exception. In 1962, the voters were not certain the military would veto Haya de la Torre; in 1963, they were. But this time, and partly as a consequence of military rule, it was unnecessary for the armed forces to take action, for their candidate, Belaúnde, won the June 9, 1963, presidential election with 40 per cent of the total vote. Now APRA cried fraud, for in two of its provincial strongholds in the north, the ballot boxes had been mysteriously stuffed with blanks. The junta ignored the charges,* and on July 28, constitutional government was restored.

Why did the military prefer Belaúnde? When the platforms of the AP, APRA, and UNO parties, and the campaign speeches of Belaúnde, Haya de la Torre, and Odría are compared, it is extremely difficult to detect differences. Haya continued to voice the APRA program for social reform, Indian integration, agrarian reform, housing, social welfare, and anti-Communism. But so did Odría and Belaúnde.† APRA's campaign thunder, so successful in winning votes, had been appropriated by both men.

Now the armed forces, also, especially the Army, were in favor of a reform program for Peru. This is no longer the military organization it was a generation ago. The officers at the top today have been witness, during their careers, to an era of growing social ferment. Up to the time of World War II, the old feudal political system had been maintained, and until then, the Peruvian social structure had been as resistant to change as any in Latin America. A tiny white oligarchy, the landed and commercial elite, consist-

---

* Belaúnde's lead over Haya de la Torre was sufficient for him to have won even if the disputed ballots had been counted for the latter.

† Belaúnde had, in fact, been an APRA deputy in Congress immediately after World War II.

ing of probably no more than fifty families, continued to control politics, as well as society and the economy, while the military periodically assisted them in suppressing popular protests and demands for change.

However, the World War II experience built up tremendous pressures for change. The political reflection of this was the 1945 election to the presidency of middle-class lawyer José Luis Bustamante, whose main support came from the *apristas*. Bustamante himself described the reasons for the change and its nature:

> New means of communication have brought us closer to the rest of the world, encouraged interchange and contacts with other countries. . . . Public education, deficient but undeniable, has activated in our people a degree of civic consciousness. . . . The multiplication of official services, and the organization of commercial enterprise on a modern basis, has suddenly created in our cities a sizable middle class. The industrial era has begun, and with it the obvious phenomenon of displacement in various areas of employment. The artisan is declining; the *campesino* is becoming a laborer . . . the urban factories attract those elements who desire to better their standard of living; they organize themselves into syndicates and form a new class of manual laborers. . . . Likewise, the Indians of the highlands migrate to work on the coasts . . . and this is bringing about the breakup of the feudal system in the highland region.*

As already noted, the stalemate between APRA and the oligarchy under the Bustamante government was ended by an Army coup and the setting up of a military dictatorship under General Odría (1948–56). But this was no traditionalist dictatorship, interested only in maintaining the *status quo*. Rather, much of the social-reform program of APRA, particularly the plans for urban reform, was adopted by Odría. Under Odría, the Peruvian Government for the first time assumed responsibility for public welfare in the capital. Social-security measures were decreed, public-housing projects were launched, and the city's organized labor groups began to see their material position improved. This was

---

* *Tres años de lucha por la democracia en el Perú* (Buenos Aires: Bartolomé U. Chiesino, 1949), pp. 14–15.

the reason that, in Lima, Odría overwhelmed both Belaúnde and Haya in the 1962 voting.

But such a program—although confined to Lima—was bound to alarm the oligarchy, and during the 1950's, it became progressively alienated from the Army. When the leading oligarchs protested the dictator's social measures, he handled them in an extremely cavalier fashion. A number of them, notably Pedro Beltrán, the editor of the newspaper *La Prensa* and premier under Prado from 1959–61, were even imprisoned for a time. The oligarchy's alliance with APRA in opposition to Odría's handpicked candidate in the 1956 elections marked a still deeper schism in the traditional military-oligarchy relationship. The election crisis of 1962 demonstrated that the break is now quite complete.

While society, politics, and the economy have undergone some fundamental changes over the past generation, the military institution has also changed. The armed forces began to become something more than a domestic *gendarmerie* from World War II onward. During that conflict, with their travels and studies in the United States, their contacts with United States military personnel, and their work on continental defense problems, Peruvian officers gradually became aware of an entire world in social crisis, and they began to appreciate more acutely the explosive problem in their own nation. Traditionally accustomed to intervene in order to save their country from what they believed to be the venality and irresponsibility of assorted civilian politicians and parties, they had also considered it natural that the Army should save the nation from a social upheaval. Odría's cautious reforms were merely the initial reflection of the Army's growing social conscience. After his dictatorship ended in 1956, the important military organization for the study of national problems became the new Center for Advanced Military Studies in Lima. This institution concerned itself, more often than not, with studies of an extramilitary nature. The military made the nation's increasingly critical social and political ferment the business of the armed forces. For example, under the junta's rule in 1962–63, the Center was involved in the preparation of both the new electoral law and the agrarian-reform decree. In effect, it was assuming legislative responsibilities in the absence of Congress.

Against this background, it can perhaps be better understood why the armed forces wanted Belaúnde and what role they now play in the Peruvian Government. Although their old grudge against APRA was sufficient grounds for vetoing Haya de la Torre, it should also be appreciated that the military and APRA are in a very fundamental sense political competitors. Both of them feel a sense of mission about resolving the nation's social problems, but in the APRA program there is no provision for military participation.

With respect to the military's rejection of Odría, the reasons were both personalistic and ideological. Odría came to the top during World War II; the present leadership is nearly a full generation younger. Odría's friendships and associations with more conservative officers were feared by the junta membership. Also, Odría's program of reform was considered too moderate. His gradualism and emphasis upon urban problems was too limited. The junta was thinking in terms of full-scale national reconstruction.

Belaúnde, then, was the candidate of the military not only because they approved of him, his party, and his reform program, but also—and more importantly—because he, unlike Haya, was willing to assign the armed services a major role in the gigantic task of national reconstruction and social integration. Belaúnde, for example, has great plans for building a national and international network of roads to tie the country together economically and to develop commerce with neighboring Colombia, Ecuador, and Bolivia. The construction of these roads will be largely the task of the Army. Similarly, the armed forces maintain a keen interest in agrarian reform, tax problems, and social welfare. Belaúnde, understandably grateful to the military for enabling him to take office as President, has assumed an almost obsequious attitude toward his benefactors. He, of course, has been astute enough to realize that no civilian political mortal can prevent the military in Peru from having their own way. It is obvious that his Army, Navy, and Air Force Ministers, General Julio Luna, Vice-Admiral Florencio Texeira, and General Carlos Granthan, are something more than servants of the executive. As heads of their respective services, they wield enormous political power.

Together with Belaúnde and his party, the military today are attempting to resolve Peru's social crisis. After more than a year in office, the Belaúnde government has accomplished virtually nothing. How long will the honeymoon last? Will the government be able to get an agrarian-reform law through a factious Congress and then to implement it in the face of the resistance of the oligarchy and in time to avert a violent social upheaval? In the present crisis situation, with the masses increasingly turning to violence, the armed forces will do what they can to save their country, if for no other reason than to save themselves. Whether they can develop their capabilities sufficiently to implement their intention to help solve the social crisis, only time, fast running out in Peru, will tell.

3. 1963: Four More to Go

Guatemala

In Guatemala City, at 10:15 P.M., March 31, 1963, a column of Sherman tanks surrounded the Casa Crema, official residence of President Manuel Ydígoras Fuentes. When a demand for entry was denied, a tank smashed through the iron gates. The President was put aboard an Air Force plane and flown into exile in Nicaragua, and Congress was dissolved. Defense Minister Colonel Enrique Peralta Azurdia assumed all executive, legislative, and judicial power.

The charge against Ydígoras: complicity with the Communists. In fact, the President had fought Communism in Guatemala for a full decade. He also provided a secret training site for Cuban exiles in Guatemala preparatory to their launching of the ill-fated Bay of Pigs invasion in 1961.

However, the Army had many grievances against Ydígoras. The President was a military man of pre-World War II vintage, whereas the rest of the Army leadership had won its spurs in the 1944 revolution against the dictatorship of General Jorge Ubico, following which the other officers of Ydígoras' generation were forced into retirement. Aside from the President, who was a general, no officer in the armed forces had a rank higher than colonel, but out of a total officer complement of 900, there were more than 500 colonels and lieutenant colonels. The lowest rank, lieutenant, had the least number of officers.

For this absurd inverted pyramid of rank, the President was

37

mainly responsible. During his five years in office, he had repeatedly tried to build up personal loyalties inside the officer corps by making spot promotions according to his personal whims and inclinations. He even appointed illiterate peasant leaders, who had helped suppress riots in the capital, to the rank of colonel. In the National Palace, many uniformed secretaries and receptionists to ministers, as well as ministers themselves, were adorned equally with colonels' insignia.

Further deterioration in the Army's morale came from the President's obvious lack of interest in improving its professional caliber. He was parsimonious about equipment for the Army, yet lavished funds upon the Air Force, which he was obviously attempting to develop as a counterpoise. The Navy consisted of three vessels, two of which were presidential pleasure yachts. The United States Military Assistance Advisory Group was impeded in its attempts to equip and develop an Army battalion into a model continental-defense unit because the President apparently feared it might be put to use against him.

Meanwhile, President Ydígoras, Commander in Chief of Guatemala's armed forces, had himself paid the highest salary of any executive in the hemispherc—$150,000 annually plus a $1-million pension fund. In addition, reports of widespread graft in the executive branch of the government were rife.

Ydígoras had been an aspirant to the presidency ever since 1950, and in the course of time, he had become quite adept in the use of demagoguery. For his 1950 vilification of the revolutionary government and its program, he was forced into exile, but he returned when the counterrevolution triumphed in 1954 and ousted the Communist-backed regime of President Jacobo Arbenz. In the election of October, 1957, following the assassination of President Carlos Castillo Armas, Ydígoras ran second to the official candidate. However, with an aroused mob and some Army support, he had the elections declared void; he then won in a new election held in January, 1958. Keeping leftist parties out of contention by questionable legal devices, he increased his congressional majority in the December, 1961, election to such an extent that the legislature became a mere rubber stamp.

But Ydígoras found it increasingly difficult to keep the opposition under control. When worker-student mobs rioted in the capital in protest against the 1961 elections, the President at first called on the peasantry to back him, then became increasingly dependent upon the armed forces for survival. In April, 1962, an all-military Cabinet was installed.

The Air Force, ungrateful for its many favors from Ydígoras, tried to take advantage of the erosion in his power. On November 25, 1962, it launched a fighter and bomber assault upon the presidential palace. After three hours of fighting, in which the Army remained loyal and in which 54 innocent civilian bystanders were casualties, the rebel airmen flew into asylum in neighboring El Salvador. The entire remaining Air Force, 500-strong, was then arrested and purged of anti-Ydígoras suspects.

The immediate cause of the Army's March 31, 1963, coup was Ydígoras' decision to allow Juan Arévalo (President in 1944–50) to return from exile to begin campaigning for the December, 1963, elections. Ydígoras had kept him abroad for five years by an assortment of legal devices and physical threats. When Arévalo announced himself a candidate for the presidency in November of 1962, Ydígoras attempted to disqualify him on grounds of Communism (outlawed in Guatemala since the ouster of Arbenz, in 1954) and of implication in the 1949 murder of the Chief of Staff of the armed forces, Francisco Arana. However, when the Supreme Court ruled on March 21, 1963, that the President had no authority to prevent the return of Arévalo, Ydígoras, determined to maintain at least a constitutional façade for his unpopular regime, had to back down. As soon as Arévalo, the overwhelming favorite to win the elections, actually did return on March 31, the Army seized the government.

The Army's opposition to, and fear of, Arévalo cannot be overestimated. And yet, ironically, it is the present Army leadership that enabled him to assume the presidency following the 1944 revolution. Why did the military become so disaffected with the revolutionary leadership? And why have they soured toward the labor-left and the whole revolutionary experiment today? A brief glance backward into recent history reveals partial answers.

Until 1944, Guatemalan politics were distinguished from those of her more turbulent Central American neighbors by their extraordinary stability. This was by no means due to Guatemala's having more democratic tendencies but rather to the superior effectiveness of its military dictators. Four strong men ruled the nation for 75 of the first 106 years of her independence—General Rafael Carrera (1838–65), Justo Rufino Barrios (1871–85), Rafael Estrado Cabrera (1898–1920), and General Jorge Ubico (1931–44). Chief features of the political milieu, all favorable for effective authoritarian rule, were extremely weak civilian political organizations, a great mass of docile, illiterate Indians held in bondage by a small landholding elite, and a rather large standing Army. The Army was really the only effective political force; it simply occupied a power vacuum.

This primitive political structure was shattered in October of 1944. The junior officers in the Army, impelled by mixed motives of professional ambition, patriotism, and social consciousness, cooperated with civilian professionals, workers, and students in deposing the generals and the oligarchs. The new revolutionary regime, led by President Juan Arévalo, a socialist intellectual, produced a rash of reform measures—expansion of educational facilities, protection for organized labor, a social-security system, state-sponsored industrialization, and agrarian reform. Its program for the military was political neutralization and professional development. The armed forces were to be made the tools rather than the masters of the state.

The traditions of a century of deep political involvement by the military were not easily broken, however. The drastic revolutionary reforms not only produced deep cleavages in civilian society, but also generated a schism in the Army. A radical faction, openly supported by Arévalo and led by Defense Minister Major

Jacobo Arbenz, began to clash with moderate-to-conservative officers, led by armed-forces Chief of Staff Major Francisco Javier Arana. Arbenz and Arana both became candidates to succeed Arévalo. In 1949, Arana was assassinated in circumstances clearly implicating Arbenz.

When the latter assumed the presidency in 1950, the revolution veered toward leftist-extremism as an energetic Communist minority began to usurp control. As a counterpoise to the disaffected Army, Arbenz and his Communist supporters proposed to develop a worker-peasant militia, but the Army, seeing this as a potential threat to their own institution, denounced the plan. In June, 1954, when a shipment of Polish arms arrived for such a militia in defiance of the Army's wishes, the civil-military crisis came to a head. By refusing to permit distribution of these arms and by refusing to put up any defense against a counterrevolutionary invasion of pro-Arana exiles, led by Colonel Castillo Armas, the Army brought the Arbenz regime and the revolution itself to an end.

Between 1954 and 1957, the combined liberation forces of Castillo Armas and the regular Army crushed the Communists and the radical left and set up a regime of enforced order and moderation in the socially disturbed country. Only lip service was paid to the original principles of the 1944 revolution. The election of General Ydígoras to the presidency in 1958 was considered sufficient assurance that they would not be implemented for five years more.

But the last year of President Ydígoras' term caused the Army considerable apprehension. As elections approached, the President himself, apparently in a bid to control the selection of his successor, embarked upon a reform course, urging such measures as revision of the tax structure and agrarian reform. Then, too, in the latter part of 1962 and early 1963, there was an increase in terrorism and insurgency. A couple of small, apparently pro-Communist, guerrilla bands appeared in the north, and Guatemala City was several times disturbed by terrorist explosions.

These were not serious threats to public order, but they did embarrass the Army. Moreover, the inefficiency and corruption of the Ydígoras Administration was becoming more and more of a public scandal, and the Army increasingly felt uncomfortable in its association with this type of government. Thus months before the March, 1963, coup, pressures were building up for an Army move against Ydígoras.

However, the coup probably would not have come except for the succession problem. Arévalo, rather than Ydígoras, was the reason for the military intervention. Arévalo, in exile, had modulated the revolutionary tone characteristic of his speeches in the late 1940's. Now he was attempting to assume the mantle of an anti-Communist, moderate, democratic reformer. But the important considerations for Colonel Peralta and the Army were Arévalo's former associations with known Communists, his past ties with Arbenz, who in exile had established a close relationship with Castro's revolution, and Arévalo's alleged involvement in Arana's murder. With rightist opposition to reform mounting, with urban terrorism and rural insurgency threatening to escalate into a serious problem, the prospect of Arévalo coming to the helm of the ship of state following elections was unacceptable to the Army. The officers simply could not afford to sit by and see their power position undermined and their careers and lives threatened.

The March, 1963, coup was undertaken to guarantee both the Army and the nation not only against Arévalo, but against social reform, as well. The present Army leadership has turned its back on the revolution it made in 1944. It got its fingers burned badly by involvement in the upsetting process of fundamental social change and reform. The revolutionary program, the civilian leadership, the workers, and the peasants, not to mention the Communists, all turned out to be threats to the very existence of the armed forces. Having eliminated these threats in 1954, they took every precaution to guard against their resurrection only a decade later. For not only do they now oppose social reform in principle, but they feel they must now protect themselves against the revenge that would surely be forthcoming if Arévalo and the labor-left should return to power. Thus, institutional self-preservation was a prime motive for the March, 1963, coup.

Many observers have interpreted the coup as an ideological reaction of the extreme right against both the threat of a return of the left and the moderate reforms of Ydígoras. They point to the oligarchy's protests against the Ydígoras government's mild income-tax and agrarian-reform laws of November, 1962, associating these with both the Air Force revolt that same month and the Army coup five months later. To reinforce this view, they point to the fact that his successor has eliminated Ydígoras' men in government and replaced them, particularly in the Cabinet, by well-known partisans of the extreme right.

However, the policies of the Peralta dictatorship thus far do not bear out such an interpretation. Colonel Peralta has used ultra-conservative civilian advisers simply because they are all that remains, the Army having forcibly removed the left and Ydígoras' supporters. But it does not follow that the military has an ideological affiliation with the extreme right. In Guatemala, as elsewhere, Army officers come from lower-middle-class families, but once they begin a military career, their overwhelming loyalties are to their institution rather than to their social class. Peralta has never been identified with any particular political ideology. His actions represent nothing more than a veto of all civilian politics. His is an almost completely negative policy. If the moratorium upon civilian political activity he enforces redounds to the benefit of the oligarchy, by maintaining the *status quo*, that is merely coincidental and not his basic intention. He has not adopted any policies that can be considered more reactionary than those of Ydígoras. Most of the latter's basic legislation, including the income-tax law, is still on the books. And just as under Ydígoras, it probably will not be enforced. Peralta's announcement in June, 1963, of a new agrarian-reform law turned out to be a reissuance of the rather meaningless and ineffective Ydígoras law, which proposed to turn over 2 million hectares of little-desired public lands to 100,000 peasant families.

The Peralta regime, then, is of the caretaker variety. It is the Army's response to a virtually complete loss of confidence in all civilian politicians and parties. It intends to administer more efficiently, root out corruption, maintain order, and arbitrate all civilian social, political, and economic crises. It has no discernible social philosophy as yet.

On assuming power, Colonel Peralta announced that the government would be returned to a popularly elected civilian President "as soon as the Army has fulfilled its mission." In exchange for recognition from Washington, he made a vague promise to hold elections sometime during 1965.* Elections for a constituent assembly were held in May, 1964, and Peralta formally scheduled presidential elections for 1965, following which constitutional government will presumably be restored.

Peralta's present difficulties arise from his attempts to reimpose the old system of political dominance by the military upon a nation that has undergone great changes since the old system was last effectively applied. For since the 1944 revolution, hitherto ignored lower- and middle-class groups have become energetic political participants. They tasted power; they launched a social revolution, and although it was perverted by the Communists and then arrested by the Army, the changes wrought by the revolution are too fundamental to be undone entirely. Although the outlawing of political parties and the suppressing of trade unions have reduced the students, the workers, and the Indian peasants to rather feeble political groupings today, Peralta cannot ignore them. Already pressures are building up from both the left and the center for a reform government. The great problem for the Army is to restore constitutional processes without allowing victory to groups unacceptable to the military. Such groups now

* When, on November 13, 1963, the Council of the Organization of American States considered holding a Foreign Ministers' Conference to discuss means of strengthening democracy in the hemisphere, Guatemala cast the only dissenting vote.

seem to include all those running from the extreme left to the right of center.

Ecuador

The date: July 11, 1963. The time: 12 noon. The place: the War Ministry in Quito, Ecuador. The orders: a tank battalion will surround the presidential palace and neutralize the presidential guard while troops rush in to arrest the President. As the soldiers entered, President Julio Carlos Arosemena fled upstairs to his private apartments and phoned nearby Army barracks for help. It was too late; they had already made commitments to the newly formed military junta.

Aroused mobs congregated in front of the presidential palace, and demonstrations against the armed forces took place in the port city of Guayaquil. Vice-President Reynaldo Varea Donosa tried to summon Congress. The resistance came too late and proved ineffective. The mobs were dispersed with a few rifle shots. Troops battered down the palace doors and seized President Arosemena. That evening he was put aboard an Air Force plane and deposited in Panama City. Vice-President Varea was also flown into exile.

Why did the military seize power in Ecuador, a country that until July 11, 1963, had enjoyed an unprecedented fifteen years of civilian rule, free and orderly elections, and constitutional government? The immediate cause, said the junta, was the shameful spectacle created by the inebriated President at a July 10 banquet honoring the visiting President of the Grace Line, which operates ships and other enterprises in Latin America. While the assembled military and civilian notables, including United States Ambassador Maurice Birnbaum, sat in embarrassed silence, Arosemena made insulting statements about United States exploitation of Latin America in general, and Ecuador in particular.

This was the last straw! Immediately after the banquet, the armed-services chiefs met and decided to depose the President, dissolve Congress, annul the constitution, and set up a military junta to rule the country. All these actions were effected the following day.

The junta readily admitted that the President's excessive addiction to the "manly vice" (alcohol) was not the principal reason for his removal—this despite their knowledge that he was not quite sober when he was received by President Kennedy in the summer of 1962, that he was unquestionably intoxicated when he received President Arturo Alessandri of Chile at the end of the year, that he had been involved in a night-club row in Quito, and that Congress had twice tried to impeach him for his hard drinking.* No, the basic reason given by the junta for ousting Arosemena was that he had been soft on Communism. It was pointed out that as Vice-President in 1961 he had made an extended visit to Moscow, that at the Organization of American States meeting in Punta del Este, Uruguay, in January, 1962, President Arosemena had joined the minority in resisting the expulsion of Cuba from the OAS and subsequently had refused to break diplomatic relations with Cuba until the Army had forced him to do so in April of 1962. He was also charged with having been insufficiently alarmed over a small band of pro-Castro guerrillas operating in northern Ecuador and with having permitted hundreds of Communists to infiltrate government agencies.

Upon closer examination, the immediate Communist threat appears to have been greatly exaggerated. There may have been some extremists in minor government positions, but the two highest officials most often charged with extremism, Arosemena's Administrative Secretary, Gonzalo Almeida Urrutia, and his Inspector General, Nicolás Kingman Riofrío, cannot be considered Communists by any stretch of the imagination. The Communist guerrilla threat was not serious; the Army had smashed one insignificant band very handily in the spring of 1962, and there had

---

* Arosemena countered these moves by asserting that he never let his drinking interfere with his executive duties, and he excoriated the "Creole Calvinists" in Congress who were critical of his private life.

been no recurrence of guerrilla activity. A more serious threat of leftist extremism came from within the armed forces itself, where in late 1962 a pro-Communist conspiracy was uncovered inside the Army's crack paratroop battalion, but Arosemena certainly could not be held accountable for this.

Another puzzling question arises. If the President was to blame for Ecuador's ills, why was Congress dissolved? Because, explained a junta spokesman, that body had "demonstrated that it was incapable of accomplishing anything."* The spokesman pointed out that excessive factionalism had produced a stalemate, and it was impossible to get congressional action on a large number of urgent reform bills. Accordingly, he concluded, the armed forces had intervened to save the country from ineffective civilian political organizations and an unworkable constitutional structure.

Congress, it is true, was unwilling to give serious consideration to the fundamental reforms urged by President Arosemena, such as tax revision and agrarian reform. Also, there was a stalemate on fiscal policy, with the Arosemena Administration running on an ever-increasing deficit and the Congress unwilling to vote the funds necessary to meet it. As a result, part of the Army, as well as other government employees, were in arrears in pay. Also, the badly divided 1962 Congress was unable to agree on passage of the armed-forces promotion lists. Certainly, there was little prospect that the 1963 Congress would be more effective.

But the charges of Communism and government ineffectiveness obscure some fundamental and complex motives behind the military intervention. To understand these, one must have some appreciation of the harrowing political crises the armed forces had to endure in the two years previous to the 1963 coup.

In November of 1961, they had felt obliged to deal with perennial President José María Velasco Ibarra. This quixotic political chameleon then sat uneasily in the presidential chair for the fourth time (his previous tenures were in 1933, 1944–47, 1952–56), and he was on the verge of being forced into exile for the third

---

* *The New York Times,* July 13, 1963.

time. Velasco, an orator without peer in the ability to arouse the Ecuadorian masses, always managed to win elections handily. His troubles began, however, when he would assume office and be unable to deliver on his campaign promises. Thereupon, his erstwhile partisans, particularly students and workers, would begin demonstrations against his government; law and order would begin to break down; and the armed forces would find it necessary to remove him. This familiar pattern was repeated again during the first week of November, 1961.

However, unexpected difficulties arose as the military chieftains divided over the succession problem. The top Army leadership was determined to get rid of Vice-President Arosemena too, but when they ordered his arrest, on November 7, the Army engineers rebelled. After a full day of hard fighting, loyal infantrymen and paratroopers were able to quell these intraservice rebels, but the following day the Air Force rebelled. The Army had installed Dr. Camilo Gallegos Toledo, Chief Justice of the Supreme Court, as Interim President, whereupon the Air Force protested that this violated the constitution, which provided that the Vice-President should succeed the President. Congress then proclaimed Arosemena President, whereupon Army tanks and troops surrounded the legislative palace. The Air Force countered by sending jets to the scene. On November 8, 1961, rocket and machine-gun fire from the planes routed the tanks and troops, thus winning a battle for constitutionalism, and Arosemena assumed the presidency.

But it soon became apparent to the armed forces that nothing had really been solved. Arosemena seemed more irresponsible than Velasco. His heavy drinking, his radicalism, his stubbornness on the Cuban problem, his "softness" on Communism, his inability to work with Congress—all this made it apparent to the armed-forces leaders that Arosemena too would have to be removed. But the great difficulty here was that nothing acceptable to the armed forces could be achieved by constitutional means. Even if the impeachment attempts should ultimately succeed, then Arosemena would be succeeded by Vice-President Varea, who was involved in a public scandal (deliberately revealed by Arosemena) over the purchase of military equipment. And if Varea, in turn, were disqualified, then the presidency would devolve upon the Speaker of the Chamber of Deputies, Jaime Acosta Velasco, the nephew of Velasco Ibarra.

As the deterioration in government became worse, with no constitutional escape in sight, an even worse threat to the armed forces and to the nation began to loom on the political horizon. From exile in Argentina, Velasco Ibarra had begun to conduct his campaign for the presidential elections of 1964, and by early 1963 it appeared that he was the strongest candidate in the field. His return to power would obviously mean a wholesale purge of the armed-forces leadership that had removed him in November of 1961. Rather than accept such a prospect, the armed forces made the unpleasant decision to violate the constitution, if necessary, to prevent the return of Velasco. There are indications that a military takeover was in the offing as early as January of 1963. Several conspiracies were nipped in the bud in the first half of 1963 by President Arosemena's shifting of key military commands. The coup itself was probably triggered as much by Velasco Ibarra's fiery radio address, prerecorded, to the nation on July 9 as it was by Arosemena's shameful performance at the banquet on July 10.

The armed-forces leadership was made much more comfortable in its unconstitutional intervention as a result of the encouragement it received from the political right. The Conservatives and Social Christians alike had been doing their utmost to rid the country of Arosemena and prevent the return of Velasco. Like the military leaders, they too feared the rise and growth of labor-leftist extremism and Communism, and had about given up all hope of stopping either by constitutional means. The Social Christians apparently hoped that their candidate, Dr. Camilo Ponce, who had held the presidency in the late 1950's, would return to power in free elections if Velasco were somehow barred, but the Conservatives wanted their own man in power and apparently believed that a brief period of military rule would provide the necessary conditions to achieve this. Accordingly, the Conservative political leaders gave every encouragement to the military to intervene.

No armed-forces split marred the July 11, 1963, coup, for the four-man junta included the heads of the three services (Navy Captain Ramón Castro Jijón, Army Colonel Luis Cabrera Sevilla, Air Force Lieutenant Colonel Guillermo Freile Posso), and the armed-forces representative to Congress, Army Colonel Marcos Gándara Enríquez. Castro Jijón of the Navy, the weakest service, was named President of the junta because he was senior in rank, but actual power resided in the Army and the Air Force. Gándara, the most articulate of the four, appeared as the junta's spokesman. He also appears to be the chief moral force and guiding spirit in the government today.

The junta soon made it clear that the armed-forces coup was something more than a negative response to an irresponsible President and an inept Congress. In the face of civilian failures, it stated, the armed forces were now going to assume responsibility for rehabilitating their country.

The immediate task was to check the Castro-Communist threat. Police and troops rounded up extremist suspects, arms were taken away from workers and students, and the junta began a systematic purge of suspected Communists in the bureaucracy.

The junta declared its firm resolve to overhaul completely the inefficient machinery of government. It pledged to reduce red tape, to curb smuggling, to bring integrity and efficiency back into the customs service, and to see to it that taxes were collected. In addition, it announced its determination to devise a political system, under an entirely new constitutional framework, that would avoid both executive irresponsibility and legislative stalemates in the future.

But even more fundamental was the junta's avowed determination to launch, for the first time in Ecuador's history, a meaningful and effective program of social reform. Implying that such reform had heretofore been stifled by stubborn conservative opposition, it promised laws for agrarian reform and for a progressive system of taxation. Once all the structural reforms had been made and the fundamental laws had been enacted, then, promised the junta, the armed forces, having fulfilled their patriotic duty, would restore Ecuador's government to the civilians and return to their barracks.

For such zeal, integrity, determination, and foresight, the military junta has been cheered both at home and abroad. Political parties and leaders are cooperating to speed the junta's interim rehabilitation work. The armed forces have solemnly promised to turn the government back to the civilians in "considerably less than two years," and they will in all probability do so, for the politicians are impatient to resume the reins of power. The foreign and domestic press has eulogized the junta leaders as a new breed of progressive military rulers, as men with a mission, men with a social conscience. Top United States officials have expressed confidence that Ecuador will now move ahead rapidly toward strengthening democracy, developing her economy, and implementing social reforms under Alliance for Progress programs.

Lest anyone feel that the millennium is already here, a look at the armed-forces role in Ecuador's past and a glance at the magnitude of the problems of the present ought to produce a certain amount of healthy skepticism.

For one thing, this is not the first time the Ecuadorian armed forces have intervened to save their nation. On July 9, 1925, a group of young officers carried out a successful coup and promised drastic reform of the government, which, they charged, was politically corrupt, administratively inefficient, and on the verge of bankruptcy. Their plans included nothing less than a complete economic, political, and social reorganization of the republic.*

---

* See General Angel I. Chiriboga, *Fuerzas morales en el ejército* (Quito: Imprenta Nacional, 1932), pp. 50–54.

Yet only minor, and ephemeral, fiscal and administrative reforms occurred. The military's efforts to bring about fundamental changes in an essentially oligarchical political system and a semi-feudal social system got absolutely nowhere. A similar nation-saving mission, with equally disappointing results, was attempted by the military junta that deposed the government of Carlos Arroyo del Río on May 28, 1944. Excerpts from the Army's proclamation to the nation at that time follow:

> The government of Arroyo has been an interminable orgy of crimes, thieving, and infamous mistakes, which have brought the country to ruin. . . . As soon as the country is pacified, a presidential election will be called, initiating an era of well-being and progress in our beloved country. . . . We, men of the people, captured the government, and set up a popular regime, the most democratic in America.*

The government that succeeded the junta in power was headed by Velasco Ibarra. Three years later, the Army unceremoniously ejected him and began all over again.

Another question arises. Do today's military leaders really possess the ability to make the kind of structural overhaul they promise? None of the four has had any notable experience along these lines. True, they have called on tax experts and agrarian specialists for help, but their political-reform advisers are leaders of the very parties responsible for the long congressional stalemate. Further, is "considerably less than two years" enough time for the junta to do very much about resolving the nation's manifold problems?

What are these problems? Politically, besides the framing of a new constitution, they involve the development of a substitute for the anarchistic multiparty system that now renders the legislature impotent. They also involve elimination of the age-old system whereby the candidate who is the most extravagant orator and the most skillful practitioner of demagoguery invariably wins presidential elections. Velasco, for example, had been the odds-on

---

* See Captain Sergio Enrique Girón, *La Revolución de Mayo* (Quito: Editorial Atahualpa, 1945), pp. 10, 54–55.

favorite to win the scheduled June, 1964, presidential election until the junta took over in July, 1963.

Ecuador is an extremely poor nation, and her problems of economic development are as formidable as those of any nation in Latin America. But these economic and political problems pale before the enormity of the social problem. The nation has one of the most anachronistic social structures in the world. A tiny landed and commercial oligarchy has maintained an uncompromising resistance to even a modicum of reform that might serve to alleviate the miserable lot of the oppressed Indian peasantry and the restless urban masses. And there is no significant middle class to bridge the social gap.

That the armed forces can do much to resolve such problems remains doubtful. It is one thing to put structural and social reforms into law. It is quite another to enforce them and make them meaningful.

Dominican Republic

At 3 A.M., Wednesday, September 25, 1963, soldiers entered the presidential residence in Santo Domingo and arrested President Juan Bosch. Three hours later, Defense Minister Víctor Elby Viñas Román announced that the Army, Navy, Air Force, and police had agreed unanimously to bring to an end the seven-month-old Bosch government. Congress was dissolved, the new reform constitution of April 29, 1963, was abolished, and the armed forces assigned executive and legislative functions for an indefinite period (but not less than two years) to a three-man civilian junta.

The armed forces explained that they were acting in accordance with their social and patriotic duty to save their country from the threat of Communism. Inasmuch as President Bosch, they explained, had stubbornly ignored their repeated demands to curb Communism, the armed forces had no choice but to depose him. Bosch was also charged with "corruption," "contempt for the constitution," "disregard of individual rights," inefficiency, and economic mismanagement.

It is true that Bosch refused to outlaw Communism and permitted partisans of Castro political freedom. In April of 1963, he permitted a small number of radical leftists to return from exile, and they promptly formed the Popular Socialist Party, but not a single one of these extremists was allowed a position in the Administration. The President, who had a long record of stanch anti-Communism, argued that the best way to fight Communists was to keep them in the open so that their hateful system and ideals could be fully exposed. To drive them underground by use of force, Bosch maintained, not only would violate the constitution but would also serve to strengthen the movement.

When extremist leaders, however, attempted to incite labor riots in violation of the constitution, the President was quick to deal with them under the law. During his short stay in office, he dismissed more than 200 Communist suspects from the public employees' association and the electrical unions. Moreover, the United States Government, which makes it its business to maintain constant surveillance over the world-wide Communist threat, appeared perfectly content with the way Bosch was handling the problem. Up to the very day of his fall, the new Dominican President was excoriated by Castro and supported by the anti-Communist, democratic governments of Puerto Rico, Costa Rica, Honduras, and Venezuela, all of whose Presidents (in addition to the then Vice-President of the United States, Lyndon Johnson) had attended his inauguration, on February 27, 1963.

Was there corruption? Admittedly, Bosch's forte was not administration, and though Bosch himself was scrupulously honest, there is every reason to assume that corruption, an age-old curse of Dominican government, had not been fully eliminated. Was there incompetence and mismanagement? Could one really tell in only seven months? Certainly the President and his chief aides, so long in exile, had little or no governing experience, but understandably they were reluctant to trust those whose experience was obtained under Trujillo. Charges of inept administrative methods and techniques were generally mingled with rightist criticism of Bosch's political and social-reform policies. The accusation that the humanitarian and legalistic Bosch had contempt for the constitution and disregard for individual rights is too patently absurd and too devoid of evidence to merit serious consideration.

In sum, the military's spectrum of specific charges against the Bosch regime appears to have little substance. If so, what were the real reasons for the September 25 coup? The answer involves some understanding of the Dominican socio-political milieu.

The ghost of the late Generalissimo Rafael Leónidas Trujillo still haunts the Dominican Republic. That infamous tyrant was master of the Dominican state for thirty-one years—from the time of his "election" to the presidency in May of 1930 to his assassination in May of 1961. He ushered his nation into an unparalleled era of political stability. Trujillo was the man United States Marines left in charge of the Dominican Army, following their efforts to whip it into a modern, efficient, professional, apolitical force that would protect incumbent governments against the curse of revolutions. And once Trujillo and the military appropriated the Dominican state for themselves in 1930, revolutions came to an end. During his long rule, the dictator showered continuous favors upon his uniformed backers, the result being that the Dominican Republic built up the most powerful war machine in the Caribbean, a military establishment far out of proportion to the actual security needs of the tiny nation. It included 17,000 troops; 12,000 policemen; light-, medium-, and heavy-tank battalions; and squadrons of fighters, bombers, destroyers, and frigates. The armed forces simply occupied their own nation. They equated any opposition to their benefactor with Communism. In effect, they stamped out all political activity. In the process, the dictator and his family bilked the nation of a goodly share of the public revenues, which they used to acquire a quarter of the nation's arable land and substantial business and industrial holdings.

Despite such graft and corruption, Trujillo also brought the nation economic progress. Stability encouraged private investment and the growth of light industry. Public works included highways, harbors, power plants, schools, and hospitals. Expanding government and industry created jobs and contributed to urban growth and to the rise of new social classes. The semifeudal socio-economic structure characteristic of rural areas was not seriously disturbed, however. Chief material beneficiaries of the Trujillo system, after "El Benefactor" had taken the lion's share, were the armed forces, the large landholders (especially the sugar producers), the rising business and industrial elite, and the growing government bureaucracy. Solidly allied with *trujillismo* until the last two years of the regime was the Catholic Church, whose control in the moral and spiritual realms was as exclusive as the dictator's was in the political.

Trujillo apparently met his end because his actions were considered inimical to the best interests of the armed forces. His persistent saber-rattling in the Caribbean and his vengeful pursuit of opposition exiles into neighboring republics discredited his regime abroad. His June, 1960, attempt to assassinate Venezuelan President Rómulo Betancourt resulted in the Dominican Republic's ouster from the Organization of American States and its diplomatic isolation in the Western Hemisphere. In this situation, the patriotic armed forces came forth to save their country. The Generalissimo was cut down by one of his uniformed colleagues.

Trujillo's death, in May, 1961, shook his governing system but by no means meant its collapse. Initially there ensued an eight-month struggle for power between the self-proclaimed heirs to Trujillo's power and wealth (men like President Joaquín Balaguer, Trujillo's brothers and son, and certain high military officials) and anti-Trujillo elements of the upper-middle and upper classes (professional and propertied men whose ancestors had governed the nation before the advent of Trujillo and who now were reasserting their right to rule). The latter element coalesced to form the National Civil Union (Unión Cívica Nacional, or UCN) party. This struggle was brought to a climax in November of 1961, when Trujillo's two brothers attempted a return from exile to take power. They were repelled by the UCN with the help of United States naval units. Thereupon, the anti-Trujillo UCN leaders promptly assumed a dominant position in the government. They forced President Balaguer to nationalize Trujillo's properties and to set up a Council of State, controlled by the UCN. The Council's right to rule was challenged by armed-forces head Pedro Rodríguez Echevarría, but his attempted coup failed in January, 1962, when a sufficient number of his brother officers refused to back him.

Thus, with the Trujillo gang removed from the scene, with the more representative Council of State in temporary control, with a promise to hold elections and set up democratic and constitutional government, the Dominican Republic was welcomed back into the Western Hemisphere family of nations early in 1962.

During the rest of that year, a people utterly devoid of organized political experience engaged in feverish activity in anticipation of the December elections. A large number of parties emerged, but by fall, it was apparent that the contest would be essentially between Viriato Alberto Fiallo with his UCN and Juan Bosch with his Dominican Revolutionary Party (Partido Revolucionario Dominicano, or PRD). By election time, it was clear that inside these two parties the nation's main social and economic-interest groups had polarized. The PRD was supported by the peasantry, urban labor, and the lower-middle class; the UCN was backed by the landholders, the business community, the Church, and the military establishment—by the forces that had prospered under Trujillo. Communist and Castroite political organizations got insignificant support. In the December 20 elections, Bosch and the PRD garnered more than 60 per cent of the total vote, trouncing Fiallo and the UCN by better than 2 to 1, and won overwhelming control of both houses of Congress.

Congress was installed, and the new President was inaugurated

on February 27, 1963. The great question then became whether
the new government would be able to implement the sweeping
reform program it had promised in the face of certain opposition
from the groups that had backed the UCN, for Bosch's reform
program threatened them all. He had promised to provide land
for the needy by dividing and redistributing the Trujillo estates
immediately, and other large holdings in due time; he had
guaranteed to raise minimum wages and to have the state assume
ownership of certain private businesses; he had opposed putting
a concordat with the Catholic Church into the new constitution
and advocated legal divorce, civil marriage, and state supervision
of parochial schools; he had planned to render the armed forces
an apolitical institution.

No sooner was Bosch in office than the attack upon his policies
began. The press, TV, and radio, all in the hands of the right,
accused him of being pro-Communist. The Church charged that
the new constitution, promulgated April 29, 1963, ignored "the
rights of God."

This immediate and intemperate antagonism toward the Bosch
government is probably best explained in terms of the UCN's
shock and surprise over the December, 1962, election results. During the first half of 1962, the UCN considered Trujilloism its
main threat, and accordingly concentrated its energies in keeping
Balaguer and his supporters under control. However, by the fall
of 1962 it was obliged to consider the sudden prominence of the
energetic Bosch and the PRD and the appeal he and his revolutionary party were beginning to have upon urban labor and the
peasantry. However, UCN leaders never dreamed that the Dominican populace would deny them their superior right to govern
the country. It was most difficult for the UCN chieftains to rec-
oncile themselves to rule by a man who, they felt, had achieved
power by demagogic manipulation of the illiterate masses.

There is some evidence to suggest that the political right was
prepared to wait for the next election before openly challenging
the Bosch government. But the new President seemed a man determined to move too fast. With respect to the landholders, he

attempted to enforce the legal limits upon the amount of land that could be held by one individual and began drawing up specific plans for distributing private lands to the needy peasantry once the Trujillo properties gave out. Businessmen were threatened by the imposition of marketing controls on staples and by the President's proposal to set up government stores to help lower living costs for the peasants and workers. Bosch also had his difficulties with United States investors. He challenged the legality of a Standard Oil of New Jersey contract awarded by the Council of State and ordered confiscation of the South Puerto Rican Sugar Company's "excess profits." The Church was threatened by Bosch's obvious determination to restrict its political activity. Here, then, was a case of the propertied and ecclesiastical elites being driven to demands for an unconstitutional resolution of political problems they faced in Bosch and the PRD. They simply could not accept a government bent upon undermining their property and institutions so rapidly.

Words could do little against Bosch's determination to bring his country sorely needed reforms by democratic, evolutionary means; guns were another matter, however. Bosch was aware that the armed forces had little sympathy for him or his policies, but somehow he believed he could persuade the military that what he was trying to do was in their best interests, too. Into the reform constitution went the following clause (Article 161):

> The armed forces are essentially obedient, apolitical, and not deliberative. The object of their creation and their existence is to defend the independence and integrity of the Republic, to maintain public order, the constitution, and the laws. They may be called upon by the Executive Power to cooperate in plans for the socio-economic development of the country.

Although there were rumblings of opposition earlier, the first serious confrontation between Bosch and the military occurred on July 12, 1963. Unquestionably influenced by growing pressures from the right, a group of colonels at the San Isidro Base, led by tank commander Colonel Elías Wessin y Wessin and a Catholic Army chaplain, issued an ultimatum to the President. They vowed to withdraw their support from his government unless he adopted a more stringent anti-Communist policy. Bosch summoned Defense Minister General Viñas Román and sped to the base to meet with the officers. He explained that he was doing everything within his constitutional power to control the Communists, that to do more extralegally would lead him down the path toward dictatorship—a path he refused to follow. While he was at it, he gave the assembled officers a lecture. He pointed out that they had been deliberating and had involved themselves in a political issue in direct violation of Article 161 of the constitution. He then ordered Viñas Román to discipline those responsible for the ultimatum. The chaplain was dismissed, but Colonel Wessin y Wessin remained and became more bitterly and openly anti-Bosch than ever. By mid-September, Wessin's challenge to the authority of the President had become so serious that Bosch called in Air Force Chief General Atila Luna and demanded Wessin's dismissal.* The issue was now drawn. The outcome was that Colonel Wessin became a brigadier general and Bosch became an exile.

Were there other, perhaps more fundamental, reasons for the military's decision to depose Bosch? Since he was allowed to assume power initially, they must have become convinced by his performance in office that Bosch's programs were incompatible with the best interests of the armed forces. For one thing, Bosch's ambitious reform, development, and welfare programs were bound to cut into the lion's share of the budget traditionally reserved to the armed forces. In this connection, it is perhaps significant that the Air Force, with its costly and complicated equipment, sparked the coup. Just a few days before it occurred, Bosch had rejected General Luna's request for a $6-million aircraft order from Great Britain.† Also, Bosch's troubles with neighboring President Duvalier had threatened to involve the Army in a distasteful fight

---

* Luna was Wessin's commander, for as a result of personal squabbles under Trujillo, the tanks were under the control of the infantry branch of the Air Force.

† On such an order, according to Bosch, Luna's commission would have been $1 million.

with Haiti. Finally, the armed-forces leaders were increasingly concerned lest the President's encouragement of organization by urban and rural labor ultimately result in new power forces that could be employed as counterpoises to the military.

When the military executed their coup on September 25, they did so confidently, for they knew that they had the support of nearly all opposition parties and politicians, business and industrial leaders, the landholders, and the Catholic Church hierarchy. In the week preceding the coup, the business community had gone on strike against the government, and the communications media had incited the people to revolt. These actions coincided with the controversy over Wessin's dismissal.

Where was Bosch's popular support when the coup came? Student and worker protests were but feeble efforts in the face of efficient antiriot measures initiated by the police. The President's party, it seemed, had remained an effective organization only until the elections and then had begun to disintegrate. It presented no challenge to the police and the armed forces. Most of the PRD leaders, it seems, had become bureaucrats, occupying themselves with technical and administrative functions essential to the reform program. In addition, Bosch had probably lost a certain measure of popular support. Jobs could not be granted to all who expected them. Also, despite the speed with which the President proceeded, many of his backers expressed disappointment that benefits from his promised reforms were not immediately forthcoming.

The question naturally arises as to whether President Bosch, had his tactics been different, might not have survived. Was he too idealistic, too inflexible? Could he have been more conciliatory with the landed, business, Church, and military elites without unduly sacrificing the basic principles of his reform program? If so, it is possible that the showdown might at least have been postponed. This, in itself, could be interpreted as a limited gain.

What kind of government did the military set up to run their country? Can one tell something about a man from his friends?

For more than a full month following the coup, the only nations that recognized the new government were Spain, Portugal, Nationalist China, and the new military dictatorship in Honduras. However, the Dominican military leaders made no attempt to camouflage their views. They announced publicly at the time of the coup that they were "turning the country into a rightist state." The three-man civilian junta they appointed to run their nation is stanchly conservative, and its Cabinet is made up entirely of Bosch's rightist political opponents.

The junta announced plans for holding elections for a constituent assembly in about fifteen months, to be followed by congressional and presidential elections in mid-1965 and restoration of constitutional government soon thereafter.

These rather vague promises, with no commitment on the future of Bosch's PRD, did not bring the expected early recognition from the United States, upon whom the Dominican Government was counting for economic and military aid. Instead, Washington exerted tremendous pressure, as a condition of recognition, to shorten the period of junta rule and to have elements of the PRD incorporated into the existing government. The junta and the Cabinet (except the Defense Minister), and the other political parties appeared agreeable to some kind of accommodation with Washington, but the military vetoed it.

The military were adamant in their decision to maintain junta rule for at least two years and to prevent the return of the PRD at all costs. They decided to go it alone, if necessary, rather than capitulate to United States pressure. This stand, of course, confirmed what nearly all observant outsiders had suspected. Despite the assurances of the junta and of the armed forces that the military have returned to the barracks, the so-called civilian "authorities" have very little actual power. The junta and Cabinet are but façades for the real rulers of the Dominican Republic today. They are the military chiefs who signed the manifestoes that deposed Bosch and installed the civilian junta. The most powerful service is the Air Force, whose planes and tanks could certainly cow the

Army and the police in the event of an interservice schism. The Dominican Navy, though probably stronger than that of any other nation in the Caribbean, is the weakest service in domestic political decision-making.

Now the political situation is getting back to normal in the Dominican Republic. The Bosch-PRD interlude is little more than a bad memory to the present rulers. They intend to see that such a situation does not recur. Almost certainly, it will not, at least in the foreseeable future. The only remaining outlet for the discontented peasantry, urban workers, and the lower-middle class is violence, and the armed forces, so long as they remain united, are more than equal to the task of containing it.

Honduras

Precisely eight days after the Santo Domingo coup, on October 3, 1963, the armed forces of Honduras re-enacted the drama in Tegucigalpa. There were only minor changes in the script. Curtain time was again 3 A.M., and the leading actors were again Air Force officers. Two squadrons of fighter planes "buzzed" the presidential palace, warning the President to surrender or be bombed out, while Army troops overcame the civil guard.

At 5 A.M., the voice of the Commander in Chief of the Armed Forces, Air Force Colonel Oswaldo López, proclaimed to the nation by radio that the "patriotic armed forces had intervened to end flagrant violations of the constitution and obvious Communist infiltration." In response to growing "popular clamor, restlessness, and anarchy," López added, the armed forces had come forth to save the nation and to forestall fraud in the presidential elections scheduled for October 13. President Ramón Villeda Morales, whose term of office was due to expire in eighty days, and Modesto Rodas Alvarado, the overwhelming favorite to succeed him, were conducted by the Air Force into exile in Costa Rica. The elections were called off; Congress was dissolved; the

1957 constitution was abolished; López proclaimed himself Provisional President.

Again, as in the Dominican Republic, the armed forces' explanation of its motives for intervening cannot withstand critical evaluation. For President Villeda, during his six years in office, had been constantly at war with the Communists. A doctrinaire democrat, he had repeatedly denounced the Communists and the Castroites, both their movements and their methods. Like Bosch, he chose to deal with them under the law, which he used effectively to drive them both from the bureaucracy and banana workers' unions. True, small Communist-Castroite guerrilla bands had operated sporadically in the countryside, but the pro-government peasantry and the armed forces had little difficulty in keeping them under control.

Also, there were political rallies and demonstrations in the capital, but these were perfectly normal in view of the approaching election. There was no apparent threat that public order would break down. The coup, of course, precluded consideration of the military's charges that electoral fraud was imminent.

It becomes clear, once Honduras' socio-political matrix is examined in brief historical perspective, that the armed forces' publicly stated reasons for intervening were essentially superficial, that these merely obscured the fundamental reasons.

Until 1954, Honduras was indeed the stereotype of a "banana republic." The banana industry was the nation's biggest, the only large-scale employer; bananas provided the chief commercial activity, the nation's only important export to the outside world. The social structure consisted of a small landholding elite, 1.5 million illiterate, politically apathetic, poverty-stricken, mestizo peasants, and an insignificant middle class. Politics were of the machine-gun variety, the plaything of the 5,000-man Army, which from World War II onward began to acquire tanks and planes. The only organized interest groups—the banana men, the landholders, and the generals—despite frequent internecine rivalry and feuding, managed to dominate the nation politically through the Nationalist Party.

The first serious challenge to the traditionalist system occurred in 1954. In that year, frustrated intellectuals and professional men stirred lower-income groups to vote for their Liberal Party and its presidential candidate, Ramón Villeda Morales. In the 1954 elections, Villeda Morales won a plurality when rival generals temporarily split the Nationalist Party. In the face of this threat from the left, the Nationalists bypassed constitutional resolution of the election results* and simply installed Vice-President Julio Lozano in the presidential palace. This action provoked Liberal Party leaders to make common cause with restless young officers, led by Major Oswaldo López. In 1956, he ousted the generals and Lozano, and headed a junta until December of 1957. Then executive and legislative powers were transferred to Villeda Morales and the Liberal Party, the overwhelming victors in the 1957 presidential and congressional elections.

The heady young military rebels, however, had no intention of surrendering the armed forces' traditional role as political arbiters or of allowing the civilian authorities to meddle, in any way, with their institution. And Villeda Morales was astute enough to realize that his continuance in office depended upon the sufferance of the armed forces. He courted their good will; he took account of their concern for public order and accordingly toned down his radical campaign promises of a rapid overhaul of Honduras' anachronistic society and institutions. He proceeded slowly, introducing modest social-welfare measures and seeking whatever cooperation he could get from the Nationalists on all plans for structural reforms in the economy, the society, and the political system. He did not challenge the traditional autonomy of the armed forces. Instead, he instructed a dutiful and equally frightened Congress to appropriate to the military the customary

* The President was required to get a majority of the votes for election, so either a run-off between the top two candidates or election by Congress was in order.

one-fourth of the national budget and to ask no questions about what they did with it.

However, it became increasingly difficult to operate a state with two autonomous political organizations—the Liberal Party and the armed forces. From the beginning, conservative officers publicly differed with the President. During 1959, Villeda barely survived four attempts to unseat him. The last of these was launched by the police, which were subsequently disbanded in favor of a new 2,500-man Civil Guard. As armed-forces leaders gravitated back to their traditional Nationalist Party base, the apprehensive President and his Liberal Party began converting the Civil Guard into a counterpoise. When Villeda Morales appointed the latter to supervise the presidential elections, the ensuing enmity between the Civil Guard and the armed forces precipitated a crisis. For the armed forces, the traditional guarantors and zealous preservers of the integrity of the country's institutions, had been deprived of one of their customary functions.

During the campaign, another threat to the armed forces developed in the person of Liberal Party presidential candidate Modesto Rodas Alvarado. Encouraged by overwhelming peasant, labor, and lower-class support, he promised to speed up the pace of change and reform. He vowed to abandon further attempts to cooperate with the Nationalists, to put teeth in the tax- and agrarian-reform programs just formulated by President Villeda and approved under the Alliance for Progress program. Alarmed moderates broke away from the Liberals and established the Orthodox Republican Party, but despite this schism, Rodas was favored to win handily. When it was pointed out that the armed forces might take issue if his program provoked resistance from the right, Rodas boasted that he was prepared to put the Army in its place,* and he made no secret of his partiality toward the Civil Guard.

---

* Rodas was deeply critical of military intervention in extramilitary affairs. He had condemned it several years previously when two civilians, suspected in the shooting of an officer, were seized by the Army, despite protests from the civil courts, and put before a firing squad.

But probably the chief factor in the coup was the personal ambition of one man—armed-forces chief Colonel Oswaldo López, the man who less than twelve hours before the actual military intervention gave public assurances that no coup would take place. Colonel López had reached the top position in the armed forces at a relatively early age, and in the tradition of Honduran politics, there was still one more step upward to the top rung in a military career, namely, the presidency of the republic. Hopefully, López saw his name put forth at the Liberal Party convention. When the party nomination was denied him, his thwarted ambition increasingly found expression in personal spite and resentment. When the Nationalist Party, preferring interim military rule to continuation of the Liberals in office, urged him to seize with bullets what he could not obtain by ballots, the temptation to do so was simply too great to resist.

The Nationalist Party leaders believed themselves the rightful governors of Honduras. Their party had long dominated national politics prior to 1956, and they felt that they had been magnanimous enough in permitting the Liberals six years of access to the treasury and the spoils of office. Their great problem was that President Villeda's rule and program had made the Liberal Party by far the most popular, and so there was no prospect for their returning to power in a free election. Instead, the dismal prospect for the Nationalist Party and its leaders was for six more years without official favors, without emoluments of public office, and without opportunities of graft—all of which might mean the demise of the party and the financial and public ruin of its leadership. This prospect was too bitter to accept. In their desperation, and in the time-honored tradition, they called upon the Army to "save the country."

Thus, what made Rodas' and the Liberal Party's political demise certain was the determination of the Nationalists to prevent a Liberal victory at any cost. Their attitude was that the Liberals had been given their chance under Villeda; it was now time for the government to revert to more responsible hands. Since this result could not be achieved democratically, the military partisans of the Nationalist Party were encouraged to use force. The coup was publicly applauded by the Nationalist Party politicians and by business and landed interests.

There is little question as to the nature of the government that seized power in Honduras on October 3, 1963. Here is clearly a regime that came into being in order to block reforms deemed inimical to the armed forces and the propertied and commercial interests. Colonel López is self-proclaimed President, exercising, like Colonel Peralta in Guatemala, executive, legislative, and judicial powers. He is advised by a nine-man Cabinet—one colonel and eight civilians with pronounced anti-Liberal views.

Known Communists and Castroites, now treated as criminals rather than political offenders, have been cleaned out of student and labor organizations. The Civil Guard has been disarmed and disbanded. The regular Army has assumed the police power, and has dealt effectively with student and labor demonstrations against the government.

How long will the armed forces remain in power? "Until the conditions that caused their move against Villeda are eliminated," said Colonel López. He estimated, at the time of the coup, that this would be about a year, following which a new electoral census would have to be taken, following which a new electoral law would have to be written, following which a constituent assembly would have to be elected to frame a new constitution, following which presidential and congressional elections would be held.

The length of time involved and the apparent lack of a political future for the Liberals prompted Washington, for a time, to suspend diplomatic relations, stop all military aid, and reassign its aid-program personnel. But this action had no moderating effect whatsoever upon López' stern plans for his country, and before the year was out, Washington recognized the new government.

4. 1964: Brazil

On the last day of March, 1964, General Olímpio Mourão, commander of Brazil's Fourth Army, stationed in the wealthy mining and industrial state of Minas Gerais, raised the banner of revolt against President João Goulart of Brazil. From his revolutionary capital, Juiz de Fôra, just eighty miles north of Rio de Janeiro, he proclaimed his patriotic resolve to rid his country of a President who, he declared, "was serving in a criminal, subversive capacity to betray the Brazilian fatherland."* Governor José Magalhaes Pinto and all the state troops of Minas Gerais promptly attached themselves to the rebel movement.

That same evening, General Amaury Kruel, commander of the Second Army, stationed in the adjacent state of São Paulo, announced his allegiance to the rebel movement and began moving tanks and troops toward Rio de Janeiro in order "to free the nation from the Communist yoke." His action, said General Kruel, was "aimed exclusively at neutralizing Communist action, which had infiltrated a number of government organs, principally in union leadership, for the sole aim of seizing power."† As in Minas Gerais, the Governor, Adhemar de Barros, and the state troops seconded the rebel action.

President Goulart called on the First Army, in Rio de Janeiro, to combat the rebels. Unhappily for the President, the main contingent sent northward to assault Juiz de Fôra defected to the

---

* *The New York Times,* April 1, 1964.
† *Ibid.*

rebel cause while those remaining in Rio de Janeiro were either tied down by naval resistance or joined forces with the President's bitterest enemy, Governor Carlos Lacerda of the State of Guanabara.*

As General Kruel advanced upon Rio, the President's position became untenable; he fled on April 1 to the new national capital at Brasília. But there he was greeted by a thoroughly hostile Congress, which threatened to impeach him unless he resigned immediately. Refusing to do so, he called upon the people to resist, then flew to his home state of Rio Grande do Sul, where the Third Army was still reportedly loyal.

But it was already too late. The President's War Minister, General Jair Dantas, was forced to resign for lack of support, and the Third Army showed little stomach for fighting the other three plus the Navy, whose ships were steaming toward Porto Alegre. Scattered resistance by striking workers in Rio de Janeiro and by pro-Goulart Governor Miguel Arraes in Recife was neutralized by efficient Army action. Thus, just two days after it began, the rebellion succeeded with very little fighting and almost no bloodshed. On April 2, Ranieri Mazzilli, President of the Chamber of Deputies, was sworn in as temporary President of Brazil, and Goulart went into exile in Uruguay. He was the seventh civilian constitutional President in Latin America to fall victim to a military uprising within a period of two years and two days.

Why did Goulart fall? His political demise was no sudden thing, nor was it entirely unexpected. The fact is that from the day he assumed the presidency at the end of August, 1961, the Brazilian ship of state had been sailing precariously through turbulent constitutional waters between the Scylla of military *coup d'état* on the right and the Charybdis of violent social upheaval on the left. The clamor for social justice, a crescendo that began immediately after World War II, under Goulart's prodding, reached a fortissimo. The social issues in Brazil were not unlike those of most Spanish-American countries, except in mag-

* Included in this state is the city of Rio de Janeiro.

nitude. While propertyless masses numbering in the tens of millions demanded land, higher wages, and more educational and health facilities, the commercial and landholding elites, a powerful minority, blocked efforts for tax reform, land reform, and social-welfare programs designed to alleviate the miseries of the lower-income groups. This they were able to do, constitutionally, through a system of pseudo democracy that enabled center and rightist factions to control Congress. The simple device for maintaining the *status quo* was a law that prohibited illiterates from voting. As a result, half the adult population was disenfranchised. Cutting across the rich-poor class crisis was a regionalist struggle between the prosperous south-central region and the poverty-stricken Northeast. In the latter area were more than 20 million peasants, organized in leagues but denied the right to vote. Reportedly, they were gravitating toward violence.

A decade prior to the 1964 coup, two key elements had come prominently into the political arena to attempt to moderate the deepening social crisis—the elected President of the nation and the country's armed-forces organization. Brazil's Presidents, particularly since 1950, were much more liberal and progressive than the various Congresses elected with them. This was because, at the national level, it became impossible to achieve victory without catering to pressures from the masses for social reform. Though illiteracy still bars most of the lower-income element from use of the ballot, a sufficient number won voting privileges after World War II so that no serious presidential candidate could ignore their demands.

However, though a reform-minded President could win office, there was very little he could do to carry out his campaign promises. This was the case not only because the conservative Congress refused to legislate the executive's programs, but also because the armed forces stood between the President and the Congress as jealous guardians of a constitutional system that had produced a stalemate with respect to nearly all legislation proposed for alleviating the social crisis.

The first major eruption of this thorny problem occurred during 1954. Getúlio Vargas had won the presidency in 1950 largely on the basis of pledges to make drastic alterations in the economic and social structure of the country. However, the congressional opposition rendered him powerless to act—at least by constitutional means. João Goulart, his radical young Labor Minister, thereupon attempted to stir the workers to action in protest, but the armed forces stepped in to block this and forced Goulart's dismissal. When the desperate Vargas, faced with the growing social crisis, thereupon attempted to maneuver his way out of his constitutional chains by encouraging strikes and mass pressures against traditional institutions, he too was ousted by the military, whereupon he committed suicide.

However, the October, 1955, elections produced a pro-Vargas winning ticket (Juscelino Kubitschek as President and Goulart as Vice-President), and this quickly brought the military back into politics. To the majority of the officers in the armed forces, Kubitschek and Goulart were unacceptable, and they tried to block their inauguration. However, War Minister Marshal Henrique Teixeira Lott narrowly staved off the military movement by seizing power temporarily and arresting the leading conspirators in all three branches of the armed services.

Thus the Kubitschek Administration was permitted to survive. Faced with adamant resistance to fundamental social reform by both Congress and the military, Kubitschek refrained from encouraging the labor-leftist agitation that had brought about Vargas' demise. Instead, he sought to deal with the social problem extrapolitically, by fostering the most energetic economic-development program in Brazilian history. And he kept the military pacified by spending more on the armed forces than on all the public-works programs combined. He did all this largely through a program of deficit financing, which produced runaway inflation and a serious financial crisis. Kubitschek's term ended with the social crisis only further aggravated.

The 1960 winning combination was Jânio Quadros, popular

governor of São Paulo, as President and Goulart, again, as Vice-President.* Quadros immediately ran head on into the same problem Vargas had faced. He could do nothing to carry out his elaborate campaign promises because of the uncompromising opposition of Congress. Whether he attempted to maneuver around the constitution and was blocked by the military guarantors of that sacred document is not entirely clear. At any event, on August 25, 1961, less than seven months after assuming office, he dramatically resigned in protest against the recalcitrance of Congress and certain unspecified selfish-interest groups. "I was overcome by the forces of reaction," declared Quadros. "I could no longer maintain public order."

Quadros' resignation promptly brought the armed forces into the streets and the proclamation of martial law. Why? Because Vice-President Goulart was unacceptable to the Army, Navy, and Air Force chiefs as President. They refused to have him as their Commander in Chief. Not only was he considered a leftist demagogue—he was visiting Red China at the time of Quadros' resignation—but the officers who had deposed him in 1954 now had to reckon with possible vengeance.

The armed forces, the traditional guardians of the constitution, were indeed placed in an embarrassing position. The three service ministers, Marshal Odílio Denys (War), Admiral Sílvio Heck (Navy), and Brigadier Gabriel Grum Moss (Air), insisted that Goulart, the constitutional successor to Quadros, resign. He refused to do so, whereupon they proclaimed that Goulart's assumption of the presidency would be "absolutely inconvenient" and made clear their intention of preventing his return to Brazil.

This action prompted a number of dissenting generals, including Marshal Lott, to demand that the constitution be respected. For this, they were arrested. However, the Third Army, stationed in Goulart's home state of Rio Grande do Sul, rebelled against the stand of the service ministers. The ministers then ordered

_____
* They actually ran on opposing slates. In Brazil, separate votes are cast for President and Vice-President.

Navy, Air, and Army units to attack the Third Army. Just at the point of battle, a compromise was worked out. As a condition of Goulart's assumption of the presidency, the military leaders demanded that the presidential form of government, which had been established in Brazil for seventy years, be changed to a parliamentary system. The idea, and the effect, of course, was to render Goulart impotent and enhance the power of Congress. Thus the military guardians of the constitution violated that document to prevent the coming to power of a man they considered inimical to their own interests, as well as to those of their country.

The nation was now plunged into worse economic chaos and political confusion. The presidential system had produced a stalemate on the social question, but the parliamentary system proved unworkable in other areas, as well, and brought a halt to nearly all government actions. It also produced an economic crisis and aggravated social tensions. Goulart, understandably, did his best to make the parliamentary system fail and to restore the presidential system. He could not move Congress, but he used his appointment powers to play politics with the military. He promptly replaced Denys, Heck, and Grum Moss with less conservative officers, loyal to himself. Command of the nation's four armies was also given to pro-Goulart men, even though officers with such sympathies were in the minority. The military consensus remained decidedly anti-Goulart.* However, Goulart's appointees soon began voicing support for his demands that a plebiscite be held to let the Brazilian people decide between the presidential and the parliamentary systems. These "nationalist-leftist" officers also began to put pressure upon Congress, which finally agreed to allow a plebiscite on January 6, 1963. Conservative officers in all three branches of the armed forces made known their disapproval, and publicly denounced the various pro-Gou-

---

* The annual elections of the Military Club provide a good barometer for determining political sentiments of Army officers. In the 1962 elections, the pro-Goulart candidate for the presidency of the club, General Pery Constant Bevilaqua, was soundly beaten.

lart commanders for engaging in the very improper function of exerting pressures for social reforms. All the same, the plebiscite was held, and the presidential system was restored by an overwhelming 5-to-1 vote.

Such action did nothing, of course, to resolve the stalemate over the social crisis. Congress continued to balk before Goulart's insistence upon an agrarian-reform law, while the President, despite his powers of appointment, could do little to budge the Army from its devotion to "constitutionalism," nor to overcome its conservatism on the social question.

However, radical leftist politicians, such as Deputy Leonel Brizola, Goulart's brother-in-law, began public criticism of the officers' political stance and urged enlisted men to exert their influence. Also, leftist generals began urging noncommissioned officers to consider their responsibilities toward the masses. One upshot of this kind of agitation was the attempt, on September 12, 1963, by 500 sergeants to seize Brasília and take over the government.

Through the remainder of 1963, the crisis brewed with no solution in sight. In the face of labor strikes in the cities and increasing turmoil in the Northeast, Goulart in October agreed with the military that a state of seige ought to be imposed, but Congress refused to consider it. Inflation began to get out of control. Demands for reform continued to be blocked by Congress. Cabinet crises became increasingly frequent. Drift and ineffectiveness characterized the government.

By year end 1963, rumors of a military coup were commonplace. There was a good deal of expectation that inevitably the anti-Goulart consensus in the officer corps would assert itself and remove the President in favor of the Speaker of the House, Ranieri Mazzilli, the next in line for the presidency. However, for a time, pronounced interservice rivalries prevented decisive military action, for in addition to the traditional Army-Navy rivalry, the Air Force had grown to a point where it, too, had an independent political position. It was more conservative on the social

question than the badly divided Army, yet it had trouble cooperating with the even more conservative Navy, largely because of a
squabble over which service should fly the planes on Brazil's
newly acquired aircraft carrier. In defiance of Air Force demands,
the Navy smuggled in its own aircraft.

There were additional indications that the traditional unity of
the armed forces was breaking down. There no longer appeared
to be a workable consensus inside their institution as to what
constituted the true national interest. The social crisis had
wrought deep cleavages inside the Army and Navy officer corps
and had aroused the noncoms of all three services. Prospects for
unity in the armed forces were further dimmed by the long
Brazilian military tradition that, in contrast to that of Spanish
America, prohibited the purging of politically dissident officers.
Thus, extreme leftists, ultranationalists—and even Communists—
continued to function freely and exert their influence.

However, in March of 1964, the policy actions of the increasingly desperate President Goulart raised, in the eyes of armed-
forces officers, a threat to their whole institution. To resist it, they
closed ranks and removed him from office.

What did President Goulart do to provoke the March 31 military rebellion? And why did he do it? It must be appreciated that
the power position of the President, especially from the beginning
of 1964 onward, became increasingly untenable as a result of the
stalemate between himself and the antagonistic Congress. With
the government hopelessly ineffective and seemingly powerless to
take remedial action, inflation became rampant (8 per cent
monthly), bringing demands from the hard-pressed lower-income
groups that prices be controlled. Concomitantly, the country
drifted toward economic collapse. Commercial debts to West
European companies could not be met, and the empty treasury
was unable to meet either long-overdue commercial debts to
foreign firms or often-extended obligations on public loans from
the United States. In this deteriorating economic environment,
both domestic and foreign capital were discouraged and a gen-

eral business slowdown ensued, all of which increased the popular clamor for the government to act.

Thus an exceedingly difficult decision was forced upon President Goulart. If he continued to do nothing, his labor-leftist support would wither away, and within a matter of months, inexorable pressures, from both right and left, would bring about his political eclipse. He could avert this ignominious end by resigning, as his predecessor Quadros had done in 1961, or he could make a bold bid, as his old mentor Vargas had attempted unsuccessfully in 1954, to break the stalemate with Congress on reform issues and thereby emerge, hopefully, with his political power greatly enhanced. Goulart chose the latter course of action. It was a desperate gamble fraught with danger for both himself and his country, for to overcome Congress, the President would have to bring the social crisis to a head. Such a move threatened civil war, but if successful, he could then try to force an alteration in the constitution, that sacred document of which the nation's armed forces were the jealous and traditional guarantors.

In early March, 1964, the President embarked on his bid to alter the basis of his political power. He demanded that the constitution be changed so that the illiterates, the disenfranchised half of Brazil's population, might have the political voice due them. He then began to stir to action the lower-income elements, both urban and rural, throughout the nation. In the second week of March, he attempted to launch, by decree, an agrarian-reform program that had long been blocked by Congress. Under authority of an old law, he ordered expropriation of all lands within six miles of all important national communications arteries—highways, waterways, and railroads. Though the expropriation was legal, the thorny matter of compensation for the owners aroused considerable resentment by property holders, for the law required cash compensation while the treasury had no funds available for this purpose. Also, this land decree seemed designed to stir the peasantry to physical action, if necessary, to obtain the properties, and the National Peasant Confederation, in the immediate wake of the decree, seemed to be encouraging just this.

At a March 13 rally of urban laborers in Rio de Janeiro, Goulart promised that the government would enforce price controls on business to protect the poor from runaway inflation. At the same rally, his intemperate brother-in-law, Leonel Brizola, urged a national plebiscite calling for the dissolution of Congress. Thus encouraged, the General Confederation of Labor threatened to launch a general strike to force acceptance of the President's reform program. Added threats to business came from the President's decree nationalizing private oil refineries and from his curbing of Bank of Brazil credits to private banks that were uncooperative with, or unfriendly to, the President's program for reform.

A highly disturbing characteristic of Goulart's drive for power was its Communist support, which he seemed to be encouraging. He began to urge legalization of the Communist Party and seemed unconcerned about the prominence of Communist leaders inside the National Peasant Confederation and the General Confederation of Labor. Communist boss Luiz Carlos Prestes seemed to be gaining increasing favor in the executive circles of government, while the President's foreign policy continued to be soft on Cuba and increasingly neutralist in the Cold War struggle.

Now the President's move to overwhelm Congress and bring the social crisis to a head roused the center and rightist opposition. Throughout rural Brazil, landholders gathered, many of them armed, to plan the defense of their property rights both against government expropriation without immediate cash compensation and against possible peasant invasion. Similarly in Brazil's major cities—in Rio de Janeiro, São Paulo, and Belo Horizonte—the great banking and industrial interests prepared to defend themselves against Goulart's political manipulation of the Central Bank's rediscounting operations and against the growing threat from organized labor. In addition, the President's use of, and cooperation with, the Communists provoked the wrath of the Catholic Church. On March 19, a half-million Catholics demonstrated in the name of anti-Communism in the State of São Paulo, and on Easter Sunday, March 29, priests exhorted Catholic women of Brazil to help save their country.

The center of resistance to the Goulart government and its policies was a cluster of the three wealthiest, most powerful, and most populous states of Brazil—São Paulo, Minas Gerais, and Guanabara, headed by anti-Goulart Governors Adhemar de Barros, Pinto, and Lacerda, respectively. Though five of Brazil's other twenty-four states joined the rebellion later, there was a marked regionalist resistance by Brazil's "big three" to Goulart's labor-leftist social-reform program. With Goulart were the poorer states of the Northeast, and, of course, his home state of Rio Grande do Sul in the far south. This 1964 revolt thus represented the same kind of geographical power struggle as that of 1930. Brazil then, as today, was characterized by extremely uneven economic development. The prosperous "big three" states, with only two-fifths of the population, accounted for two-thirds of the national income, while the depressed Northeast, plagued by shortages of power, communications, and industry, fell further and further behind. The regionalist issue revolved around the question of responsibility of the "big three" for financing nationwide economic development. They now paid more than half of all federal taxes and were understandably reluctant to bow to Goulart's demands that they contribute more.

This complex power struggle between the President, the labor-left, and the North and South on the one hand, and the Congress, the center-right, and the Minas Gerais–São Paulo–Guanabara complex on the other, pushed Brazil to the verge of civil war by late March, 1964. It was averted only by the timely intervention of the military, through their March 31–April 2 rebellion against the President and his backers.

Although, as indicated earlier, the consensus in the officer corps was anti-Goulart, the military, until March of 1964, were inclined to await expiration of Goulart's presidential term in

1965 rather than remove him from office by force. But Goulart's actions in March gave rise in the officer corps to the gravest concern for their own institutional welfare. His deliberate intensification of the social crisis, his efforts to change the constitution, the demands of his backers that Congress be dissolved and that the constitutional ban on immediate re-election of Presidents be lifted—all these raised disturbing questions in military circles about Goulart's real intentions. Was he aiming to maintain himself in power beyond 1965? Was he trying to re-establish a Vargas-type dictatorship like that of the 1930–45 era? Then, too, the center-rightist resistance surely meant that unless Goulart were stopped, public order, which the armed forces have a constitutional duty to preserve, would almost certainly break down. Increasingly, the anti-Goulart civilian opposition urged the armed-forces leaders to assume their constitutional responsibilities and save the country from a President who, in their eyes, was bent on destroying it.

The tiny spark that kindled the revolt was a speech by Marine Corporal José Anselmo to the Sailors' and Marines' Association in behalf of Goulart's reform policies. Anselmo was promptly arrested by his superiors for violation of the military code, which prohibits political activity by enlisted men. Thereupon, in protest, 425 of Anselmo's colleagues assembled on March 25 inside the Metallurgical Workers' Union building and declared a sit-in strike. They demanded social reforms for the country and better food and political rights for enlisted men. Navy Minister Admiral Sílvio Borgas ordered arrest of the leaders of the mutiny and disciplinary action against all the strikers. Thereupon Goulart replaced him with a new Minister, Admiral Paulo María da Cunha Rodríguez, and the mutineers were all pardoned on March 27.

For this action, Goulart was destined to lose his office. Here, clearly, was an obvious case of the President's undermining the military institution by deliberately encouraging insubordination by enlisted men. On March 29, 2,000 naval officers assembled at the Naval Club in Rio and decided to issue an ultimatum to President Goulart insisting that the mutineers be disciplined. That same evening, Army officers assembled at the Military Club, with the memory of the sergeants' revolt in September of 1963 still fresh in their minds, and decided to back the Navy against the President.

Confronted with the Army-Navy officers' ultimatum, President Goulart went before a nationwide television audience on the night of March 30 and agreed to permit an investigation of the mutiny, but at the same time, he ordered an investigation of those officers who demanded that the striking enlisted men be punished. This was more than the armed-forces leaders could bear. They refused to submit any further to presidential undermining of control of their own institution. The following day, they launched their rebellion.

Brazil's labor-leftist President was deposed by the center-right civilian opposition, as well as by the officers of the armed forces. The former apparently presumed this was just another military intervention in the traditional pattern (such as those of 1945 and 1954), in which after the President had been removed, the armed-forces leaders of the coup would promptly withdraw, and the matter of presidential succession would be resolved by constitutional processes.

The victorious military command, however, had no intention of rescinding power to the civilian politicians. In their view, the 1964 crisis was the second in a decade wherein the nation had been brought to the verge of disaster by demogogic, opportunistic, civilian politicians. Vargas in 1954 and Goulart in 1964 had brought political chaos and economic dislocation, had nearly produced social disintegration, and had undermined the morale and discipline of the nation's armed forces. Rather than risk still another repetition of widespread deterioration in the future, the military leaders made the unprecedented decision to remain in power at least until such time as the nation was purged of the sinister and corrupt influences that, in their eyes, had been attempting to destroy it. They insisted that they were going to "complete the revolution" and "to return Brazil to traditional Christian and democratic ways."

Accordingly, in the immediate wake of the revolutionary triumph, the heads of the three armed services demanded that Congress elect Army Chief of Staff Marshal Humberto Castelo Branco, key strategist of the anti-Goulart revolution, to serve out the remainder of Goulart's term, to January 31, 1966.* While awaiting Congressional action on this mandate, the armed forces began rounding up Communists and extremists. More than 7,000 people were arrested in the week following the coup.

On April 9, the military command issued an Institutional Act, a decree that in effect proclaimed for themselves dictatorial powers. Under the act, all constitutional guarantees were suspended in order to allow the armed forces to proceed with their purge. It was drastic and rapid. They promptly removed forty-four "pro-Communists and extremists" from Congress (about one-tenth of the membership), the bulk of these being members of Goulart's Labor Party, the largest in Congress. To guarantee the military rulers against Congressional obstructionism, the Institutional Act provided that any bill the President submitted to Congress would become law within thirty days, and that all financial and budgetary matters were to be under Presidential control.

The second order of business was the purge of all pro-Communist and extremist public employees. The Labor and Education ministries were "cleaned out"; two university presidents were removed; military officers assumed control of the major unions. At the state level, a large number of officials, including the pro-Goulart governors of five states, were removed. Last but not least, the armed forces were purged. More than 150 "politically minded" (that is, pro-Goulart) officers, including 21 generals and admirals, were retired from active duty.

To ensure against the return to public office of elements unac-

* The constitution rules the Army Chief of Staff ineligible for election to the presidency for ninety days following his retirement from the service.

ceptable to the military command, more than 200 prominent public men were divested, under the authority of the Institutional Act, of voting and office-holding rights (either elective or appointive) for a period of ten years. Those proscribed politically included former Presidents Goulart, Kubitschek, and Quadros, Communist chief Luiz Carlos Prestes, Peasant League leader Francisco Julião, Northeast Development Agency head Celso Furtado, Pernambuco Governor Arraes, Deputy Brizola, and Justice Minister Abelardo Jurema. By no stretch of the imagination was the purge merely anti-Communist, for it included anyone the military command happened to disapprove of; more of those affected were non-Communists than Communists.

On April 11, 1964, the Congress elected Marshal Castelo Branco as President. He apparently sees his main task as rooting out Communism and extremism and cleaning up civilian political inefficiency and corruption. His stated aim is "to moralize our institutions." He pledges to tackle the problem of inflation and promote orderly economic development, relying heavily upon private enterprise, both foreign and domestic. In international relations, his line is more pro-Western, less neutralist, more anti-Castro. On the socio-political problem, the stated approach is moderate. Goulart's agrarian-reform plans have been rejected, but a new plan has been promised. Also rejected is a policy of conservative reaction to deal with Communism and labor-left extremism. Presidential elections were promised for October, 1965, with the government to be returned to the civilian authorities on January 31, 1966; but in July, 1964, the military announced that elections would be delayed a full year, i.e., until October, 1966.

The military leaders of Brazil have truly assumed an awesome and unprecedented responsibility. The government has been taken out of the hands of the civilians for the first time since the early days of the republic. Though Congress and the courts continue to function, President Castelo Branco and a shadow junta, consisting of the heads of the three armed services and the nation's four armies, are making the major decisions. Whether they will be able to reconstruct their nation in those critical social, economic, and political realms where the civilians have failed so miserably remains to be seen.

President General Castelo Branco, to judge from his past record and recent attitudes and statements, probably has every intention of returning power to the civilian authorities on schedule. However, there is already a strong move within the officer ranks to seat another military man in the presidency when Castelo Branco's term ends. There is also increasing military pressure to bypass the presidential elections and to select Castelo Branco's successor by military consensus. The Brazilian armed forces may well find, as has been the case in so many other Latin American countries, that the assumption of governing power is a far less complex matter than the release of that power.

Prior to 1954, the role and mission of the Brazilian armed forces was firm and clear. They had simply to guarantee public order and constitutional processes, and to achieve both, it was necessary to intervene briefly only once (in 1945) in the first half of the twentieth century. In the past decade, however, there have been four interventions (1954, 1955, 1961, and 1964), all of them reflections of the ever-intensifying socio-political crisis. Increasingly, the military's concern over Communism and over the political thrust of the labor-left has made its role in maintaining public order incompatible with that of preserving the constitution. In 1955, the pro-constitutionalist forces barely won out; in 1961, they suffered a partial defeat (as the constitution was temporarily changed); and in 1964, in the aftermath of the revolution, they were overwhelmed completely by the military advocates of public order.

The parallels between the Brazilian military intervention at the end of March, 1964, and Argentine military intervention of exactly two years previous are striking. In both cases, the President was ousted for gravitating toward the labor-left. In the aftermath of the coups, leftist political leaders were prevented from exercising the powers they had won in free elections. The military in-

terveners in Argentina saw to it, by the use of force and various
legal devices, that the labor-left would be kept from power and
that right-of-center politicians would dominate when constitutional processes were restored. Certainly there is every indication
that Castelo Branco and his shadow junta are going down the
same path.

But although the personalities who agitated most in behalf of
rapid political change and reform have been removed from the
scene, the issues themselves remain. They have been avoided, not
settled. They have been perverted and confused by the admixture
of the Communism issue, but inevitably the social-reform issue
will return again to plague the nation. Beneath the present political surface, a crisis continues to ferment of the greatest potential
danger to the entire hemisphere, of greater future moment, surely,
than the present threat posed by Castro's Cuba. For Brazil
envelops half the entire South American continent and contains
a third of Latin America's 225 million people. Thus, what happens there is bound to have deep repercussions elsewhere.

5. Military Acquiescence in Social Reform

Venezuela

Just recently in Venezuela, a nation whose political history up to the year 1958 could be told in the lives of its military dictators, there was a truly remarkable achievement: President Rómulo Betancourt served out an entire constitutional term of office (1959–64). He was the first elected civilian President in the nation's entire history to do so.

What made his feat all the more remarkable was that he served at the head of a government genuinely devoted to the theory and practice of democratic political processes, of well-planned, government-sponsored economic development, and of sweeping social changes, including such fundamental reforms as redistribution of liquid wealth through a progressive tax system and of landed wealth through a meaningful agrarian-reform program.

Venezuela is the only country in South America where a democratic social revolution, such as is outlined under the Alliance for Progress program, is well advanced. Since the chief impediments to such an undertaking have been the armed-forces organizations in most of the rest of Latin America, the reasons for the Betancourt government's success in keeping skeptical generals from intervening merit close consideration. They may provide lessons to other civilian governments for dealing with their military organizations.

The military dictatorship of General Marcos Pérez Jiménez (1948–58) was one of the most brutal, corrupt, and irresponsible the nation had ever known. He outlawed all civilian political parties and persecuted their leaders. He crushed the independent labor movement, the press, and the universities. He brought to an end all social-reform programs and squandered most of the government revenues in spectacular construction projects. He lavished funds upon the armed forces, building them, for example, the most luxurious and expensive officers' club in the entire world, and he and his associates stole hundreds of millions of dollars of public funds.

This regime finally collapsed in January of 1958, following widespread civilian resistance and defections in the armed forces. The ruling clique of generals in the Army was increasingly resented by officers of lesser rank, position, and privilege. Then, too, the Air Force and the Navy grew ever more restless under a regime run largely by and for the Army. Also, during the 1950's, many middle-rank officers, from all three services, had received advanced training in the United States, where they absorbed certain notions about a responsible military organization and responsible government. In early January, the Air Force bombed Caracas, and several weeks later, the Navy revolted; this, along with a general strike, brought the dictatorship to an end. A junta, headed by Navy chief Rear Admiral Wolfgang Larrazábal, governed for one year pending elections and the restoration of constitutional processes.

President Betancourt assumed power in February, 1959, following his victory in the December, 1958, elections. From the very beginning, he did his utmost to convince the armed forces that he was sympathetic to their institutional needs and aspirations. In his frequent messages to the nation, he repeatedly praised the officer corps for its apolitical, professional comportment, for its loyalty, and for its patriotism. Ever aware that the military had the power to depose him, the President questioned neither the traditionally liberal defense budgets, nor the purchase of jet aircraft and modern arms for the mythical role the military was preparing to play in defending the country against unspecified external threats.

He rarely missed a military ceremony or parade and was liberal with promotions and fringe benefits.

The President also used his not inconsiderable powers of persuasion. He pointed out to the officer corps the advantages a constitutional system had for their vested institutional interests, the benefits to their professional growth and development that democracy could bring. On the other hand, he warned them that their whole institution might be annihilated by an aroused populace, as had happened in Cuba, should they attempt to reimpose a dictatorship of the Pérez Jiménez type. He repeatedly outlined for them the Castro-Communist strategy for Venezuela, namely, to break down law and order by terroristic acts and thus provoke a coup, and the installation of a military dictator. The latter was designed to serve as a mere straw man, against whom, in the second stage, the Castro-Communists would then rally the entire population to provoke a violent social upheaval. In this process, the armed forces were scheduled for destruction. Thus, explained the President, for the military to intervene politically was to play directly into the hands of their worst enemies.

While the President's arguments were not always convincing, he was able to benefit from, and to take advantage of, interservice rivalries to enhance his own power position. The Army, from which the danger of a rightist coup threatened, was in temporary public disgrace because of its close identification with the Pérez Jiménez dictatorship. The Navy, on the other hand, was in the ascendant, for it was the heroic service of the 1958 revolution. However, it posed a potential leftist threat to President Betancourt. Although Admiral Wolfgang Larrazábal, who had been supported for President in the 1958 elections by the Communists and the Caracas mobs, was sent as Ambassador to Chile, his brother, Admiral Carlos Larrazábal, and his brother-in-law, Admiral Sosa Ríos, retained command of the Navy. Also, the Navy's new 5,000-man Infantería de Marina (Marine Corps) was resented by the infantry branch of the Army. The President maneuvered between the embittered Army and Navy by siding with the more moderate, less political, Air Force. For example, during most of Betancourt's term, Air Force Brigadier General Antonio Briceño Linares served as Defense Minister. One further complicating factor was the National Guard, a proud, highly professional, nearly autonomous organization, which was often at odds with the Army.

During Betancourt's first three years in office, the military threat to the government came from rightist elements in the disgruntled Army. During 1959, rumors of a coup were common, several conspiracies were discovered, and a rather large number of suspect Army officers were transferred, passed over for promotion, or simply dismissed. In April of 1960, a former Defense Minister made a bid for Army support and launched an unsuccessful invasion from Colombia. During 1961, several coups were attempted by Pérez Jiménez' associates. A former head of the National Guard led an unsuccessful attempt in May. The following month, other retired rightist officers seized the Barcelona Army garrison in eastern Venezuela, but they were quickly crushed in a combined Army-Navy-Air assault.

During 1962, hitherto dormant leftist military rebels awoke. In May, a Navy Marine Corps battalion and some National Guard units, in cooperation with Communist and Castroite elements, seized the port of Carúpano in eastern Venezuela and announced themselves in rebellion against the Betancourt government. No sooner had loyal Army and Air Force units, in a pitched battle, broken this resistance, than another Marine Corps battalion, also in collusion with the extreme left, seized the naval base at Puerto Cabello and called for a general uprising. This insurrection was broken only after a bloody battle in which there were hundreds of casualties. The victors were the Army tank battalion and the Air Force fighter squadrons to whose superior firepower their Marine Corps brothers-in-arms finally succumbed.

With the back of the military rebellion broken, the challenge of the extreme left then continued in the form of a Castro-Communist civilian terrorist organization, the Armed Forces of National Liberation (Fuerzas Armadas de Liberación Nacional, or FALN), which was determined now to provoke a rightist military coup. During 1962, FALN terrorists killed or wounded more than eighty policemen, burned seventy-five buses, robbed numerous business establishments, and performed repeated acts of sabotage in the oil fields. Their antics in 1963 included the hijacking of a freighter and airliner, the usual bombings, burnings, murders, and robberies. When this failed to provoke a coup, the armed forces themselves became the objects of direct attack. In a desperate effort to stave off elections, the FALN attempted to assassinate Defense Minister Briceño, murdered five National Guardsmen, and kidnaped a colonel attached to the United States Military Mission.

This terrorism had its desired effect, at least partially, for the nervous military demanded that Betancourt take stronger action—make wholesale arrests and imprison suspects, lest law and order break down completely. The President, however, refused to act outside the law and the constitution. Retirements, transfers, and promotions were used to keep the military in line during 1962 and early 1963, but when the terrorist assaults began to be directed against the armed forces in the fall of 1963, the President was forced to take an action of questionable constitutionality. On September 29, 1963, he ordered the mass arrest of hundreds of leftist extremists; turned over Communist and Castroite Senators and Deputies, who had been using their congressional immunity to incite violence and rebellion, to military courts for trial; and permitted the troops to come into the streets to combat the FALN. This partial capitulation to military pressures was the price Betancourt was obliged to pay for his own survival, as well as for the survival of constitutionalism and democratic processes.

On December 1, 1963, with the armed forces attempting to preserve order and the FALN threatening to shoot anyone who went to the polls, with the Communist and extreme-leftist parties suspended by the government, presidential and congressional elections were conducted. Raúl Leoni, of Betancourt's Acción Demo-crática party, won a plurality in the presidential voting, although the incumbent Administration's coalition broke down soon after the elections.

President Leoni was inaugurated on March 11, 1964. It was doubtful whether he might be as astute a maneuverer among the military as Betancourt had been. Also, although the latter had done much to heal the traditional breach between civilian and military elements in Venezuela, the age-old suspicion of officers toward civilian politicians, and especially toward reformers, was far from obliterated. It would take more than five years to eradicate the tradition of more than a century of political inclinations on the part of Venezuelan officers.

On the other hand, Leoni may now be able to continue the successful Betancourt methods for dealing with the generals and admirals. Though they are far more conservative than his moderate-leftist, reform-minded government, the officers are hesitant to intervene, if for no other reason than that there is no political organization in existence in Venezuela to the right of the present one to whom they might conceivably transfer power. Also, it is quite apparent that the armed forces, as a result of the public discredit and antagonism heaped upon the Pérez Jiménez dictatorship, have little stomach today for attempting to rule the nation themselves. Most top officers now appear to understand that military rule is probably the surest way to provoke the outright destruction of their entire organization by a thoroughly vindictive, antimilitary civilian populace.

El Salvador

Tiny El Salvador is a kind of microcosm in which the common political, social, and economic problems that plague all of Latin America are both simplified and magnified. The armed forces are overwhelmingly dominant politically. Since 1931, this nation has had no President who was not also an Army officer. Society is highly stratified. Fourteen families own the lion's share of the arable land, mostly given over to coffee production, while 250,000 peasant families try to eke out an existence as tenants on the large estates or on marginal holdings of their own. In this predominantly agricultural economy, the population density is 125 per square mile and increasing by more than 3 per cent annually.

What is unique about this country today is that it is being governed by a military man, Colonel Julio Rivera, devoted to a program of democratic freedom, economic development, and social changes. Here is the only country in Latin America in which the armed forces organization is both leading and supporting the nation along the pathway of democratic, evolutionary, social revolution.

El Salvador's Army attempted a reform mission once before. In December of 1948, a group of majors seized power from the generals and announced a grand program for revolutionary social change. Elaborate schemes were drawn up, but implementation got nowhere in the face of the oligarchy's resistance. Accordingly, during the 1950's, the reform movement rapidly lost its zeal as the military rulers paid maximum attention to their institutional and personal needs while virtually ignoring those of the poverty-stricken masses.

However, the growing popular ferment eventually took the form of pro-Castro civilians joining with extreme-leftist military officers to conduct a successful coup on October 26, 1960, against the corrupt and tyrannical government headed by Colonel José María Lemus. The new regime was much too radical for the majority of the Army officers, however. Led by Colonel Aníbal Portillo and Colonel Julio Rivera, they staged a countercoup on January 24, 1961.

For the next one and one-half years, these two colonels governed the country by decree through a moderate directorate backed by the armed forces. These men were essentially resurrecting the revolution of 1948, but this time, they began to put real teeth into the social-reform program. After dealing with the Communists and Castroites, the new junta promised to set up democratic constitutional government. To this end, it sponsored an official party, which won all the seats in the constituent assembly and produced a new democratic constitution in early 1962. Meanwhile, during 1961, pro-labor decrees were issued concerning maximum hours, minimum wages, and improved diets for the undernourished agricultural workers. When the landed oligarchs protested, they were greeted with a decree for a graduated income tax, with rates running up to 76 per cent.

The reform junta—attacked by both the extreme left, whose thunder it was stealing, and the oligarchs, whose wealth it was threatening—went determinedly ahead with its manifold reform programs. Elections were held in April, 1962, but the opposition refused to participate against the overwhelmingly popular candidates of the official party. Thus on July 1, 1962, Colonel Julio Rivera was inaugurated as President of El Salvador for a five-year term. He was supported by a National Assembly in which the official party, the National Conciliation Party (Partido de Conciliación Nacional, or PCN), had all the seats. Furthermore, a majority of the armed-forces officers backed him.

During 1962 and 1963, the Rivera government pushed forward with its reform programs. Castro-Communist extremists, who set off bombs and promoted student and labor riots, were dealt with harshly but within the law. Rivera guaranteed freedom of the press and brought more integrity and fiscal responsibility into government. Meanwhile, the National Assembly began enacting into formal law the emergency decrees of 1961—a new labor code, income-tax legislation, and social-welfare measures.

During 1963, as the pace of social reform and democratic progress speeded up, so did the resistance to it from the right, and as a consequence, it became increasingly difficult to preserve public order. By late 1963, there was a sharp increase in the restlessness of military officers inclined toward intervention and toward bringing the reform experiment to an abrupt end, such as had happened in neighboring Honduras.

In the face of the growing unwillingness of conservative sectors, both civilian and military, to accept such a large dose of reform all at once, President Rivera moderated his programs considerably during 1964. He watered down his demands for more progressive tax legislation and became less adamant and less impatient about the passage of a meaningful and effective agrarian-reform law. As a consequence, though leftist criticism mounted, the regime became more stable politically during the first half of 1964.

All things considered, President Rivera's record to date has been commendable. His successes include the persuasion of domestic and foreign capital to make new investments, the passage of a progressive labor code, the implementation of Alliance for Progress program objectives, and the establishment of an atmosphere of real political freedom.

Yet the Rivera government still has a long way to go. There seems little prospect of an agrarian reform that will break up the large estates and redistribute land to the peasantry. Also, many of the reform laws relating to taxes and social welfare have yet to be implemented effectively. Also, although the gross national product increased significantly in 1962 and 1963, serious obstacles to the continuance of economic growth must still be overcome.

6. Military Intervention Today: A Comparative Analysis

The Military Branch of Politics

To understand the nature of military intervention in Latin America today, it will help to dispose first of a prevalent myth. This is the notion that the armed forces are primarily a military institution. That this notion is erroneous becomes clear when their actual functions are scrutinized. There are two—and only two—legitimate military functions for an armed-forces organization to perform, namely, to defend the nation against external aggression and to defend the government by preserving internal order. However, in Latin America not only is there no real threat of extracontinental aggression, but the armed forces are totally unprepared to defend against it should it come. What is more, Latin American armies will not fight abroad. They showed no inclination for supporting joint action in Korea in 1950 (except for Colombia), in Guatemala in 1954, or in Cuba today. Since the turn of the century, defense of Latin America has been a task assumed by the United States, and the latter is pledged to assume that task today.

As to protecting incumbents against internal disorders, more often than not, when civilian opposition to a constitutional government arises, the military, rather than come to the defense of such a government, will generally supplant that government with one more conducive to the maintenance of law and order. Furthermore, in the eyes of the military, the government exists to defend the armed forces, rather than vice versa. When this inversion of the military function occurs, as it does in most of Latin America today, then that function becomes purely political.

What of the military paraphernalia—the aircraft carriers, the destroyers, the jet fighters, the bombers, and the tanks? What are they for? Obviously, they are not for defense against Russia, or even Cuba. This hardware is sometimes purchased to keep pace with one's neighbors. For example, there is the struggle for supremacy among the Peruvian, Ecuadorian, and Venezuelan Air Forces and among the Argentine, Brazilian, and Chilean Navies, but national pride and jealousy, rather than preparations for future wars, explain the purchase of such equipment. For all the nations of Latin America are allied militarily under the 1947 Inter-American Treaty of Reciprocal Assistance (the Rio Pact), and the peace machinery of the Organization of American States has, in effect, outlawed war within the hemisphere.

In fact, the military hardware is exclusively for internal use and is utilized by the armed forces mainly for political rather than military functions. These arms, particularly the tanks and planes, were used to topple seven popularly elected governments between March 29, 1962, and April 2, 1964 (an average of one every 105 days), and in the aftermath of the coups, to cow the deposed regimes' student, labor, and peasant supporters.

Brandishment of these arms has been generally sufficient to enable the military to seize power from the civilian authorities, but the only arena in which the arms are actually employed in battle is against rival services within the country, such as the Air Force versus the Army in Ecuador in 1961 and in Guatemala in 1962, the Air Force and Army versus the Navy in Venezuela in 1962, and the Air Force versus the Navy in Argentina in 1963. In addition, these arms may be employed in intraservice fighting, particularly within the armies, such as in the case of the engineers versus the infantry in Ecuador in 1961 and the cavalry versus the infantry in Argentina in 1962. The acquisition and use of arms for conducting internecine service warfare within a country can hardly be considered a legitimate military function, for the various services, or branches thereof, invariably fight over political issues—constitutionalism in Brazil and Ecuador in 1961, and also in Guatemala and Venezuela in 1962, and elections in Argentina in 1963. All these matters were resolved in favor of the military faction having the greater number of units of effective firepower. That the issues themselves are resolved with bullets rather than ballots does not obscure their essentially political nature.

In urban centers, of course, problems of internal order are dealt with by the police, and the police function is one most military men consider degrading. In rural areas, expanded guerrilla activity, abetted by the new revolutionary thrust emanating from Castro's Cuba, is a possibility, and should this become a serious problem, a legitimate military function of preserving internal order would develop. However, the armed forces have put only a tiny fraction of their energies and equipment into preparations for antiguerrilla warfare. They consider this also rather ignoble police-type work. Thus far, the counterguerrilla commandos have been much more interested in political operations in the capitals, such as in deposing President Prado in Peru and President Bosch in the Dominican Republic.

In terms of political institutions, there is no civilian political force or combination of forces able to compete with the armed forces. Once that institution makes up its mind on a given issue, nothing can prevent it from having its way. This is largely because the military has arms, a monopoly on the means of violence, and thus the incontrovertible argument of force on its side. But it is also because the military possesses an organizational structure far superior to that of any civilian political party. Its centralized command, its hierarchical structure, and its disciplined membership make it capable of acting with complete unity. However, the recent armed-forces schisms have served to weaken somewhat the military's heretofore customary advantages in weapons and organization.

The armed forces hold that they have a legitimate political mission above that of the government. Their first allegiance is to the nation and to the constitution, as they interpret it, rather than to the ephemeral civilian politician who happens to occupy the presidential chair at a given moment. Thus, the military's custodianship of the national interest, a heritage from the wars for independence, makes its political involvement inevitable.

Normally, the armed forces will support the duly elected civilian government, but the moment the situation departs from what they view as normal, they begin to re-examine their position. If public order threatens to break down as a result of growing opposition to the policies of the incumbent government, then the military feels a constitutional duty to intervene, usually only temporarily, to provide the nation with a more viable administration. The armed forces always disclaim any desire to exercise political power themselves; they wish only to guarantee that the civilians who exercise it are doing it properly in the true national interest and are not perverting their functions. Perversion of the governing function includes, in the eyes of the military, any actions inimical to the interests of the armed forces, such as any humiliation, material weakening, and moral undermining of the armed-forces establishment.

Military intervention in Latin America, however, is something more than crude praetorianism. The generals are not capricious ogres whose only interests are destroying democracy and raiding the national treasury. On the contrary, ranting and raving about the curse of malevolent and irresponsible militarism is considered puerile and old-fashioned by sophisticated civilian politicians. Armed-forces officers, of course, view themselves as sincere patriots. Their intervention, they believe, is always in the national interest—to save their country or to protect their institution, which they consider the very embodiment of nationhood. In sum, the armed forces are an organization with an independent position on all the major political issues.

Military Involvement in the Social Revolution

A true understanding of the recent military interventions can proceed only from some appreciation of the social crisis that envelops Latin America. The relatively stable societies of the nineteenth century have suffered severe tensions and social cleavages. Previously static economies have undergone dynamic processes of growth and development. Hitherto apathetic lower- and middle-income groups have begun to enter the political arena. Meanwhile, modern communications and technology have begun to break down the area's former relative isolation from world affairs.

This process of political, economic, and social change was already in motion at the time of World War I, but it was speeded up by the Great Depression and the ideological impact during the 1930's of socialism, Communism, fascism, and the influence of the New Deal.

World War II brought the developing social crisis to a head in most of Latin America. By that time, the class structure had been substantially altered and the economies drastically changed. This was the result of a determined drive for industrialization, a rural exodus to the cities, the rise of an industrial proletariat, the growth of labor unions, and the participation of ever-larger middle-class groups in business, government, industry, and the professions. And yet in the face of these very obvious and deep-seated social and economic changes, governments continued to remain in the hands of oligarchic leaders and social groups unrepresentative of the people and ill-suited to cope with urgent national needs.

Paralleling the anachronistic civilian political structures were badly out-of-date armed-forces organizations. The latter were still commanded by old-fashioned barracks-trained generals, superannuated generals with bureaucratic mentalities, generals devoid of an appreciation of the training, equipment, salary, and promotion needs of a modernizing army. This condition was particularly frustrating to the majors and colonels. They were products of the new military academies. Further, they were influenced by advanced schooling in Europe in the late 1930's and by the training provided by United States military missions in Latin America during World War II. These also were officers with social and political consciences—as well as personal ambitions—who felt a duty to save their nations from irresponsible and outmoded leadership.

Therefore, it was only natural that military foes of the *status quo* should join with those in the civilian sector in revolutionary movements designed to break through the oligarchic dikes and usher in a flood of political and social change and reform.

The first such breakthrough occurred in Argentina under the leadership of Colonel Juan Perón in 1943. The following year, traditionalist governments were overthrown in Ecuador and Guatemala by popular revolutions led by young officers. In 1945, the same thing occurred in Venezuela. The revolutions in El Salvador in 1948 and in Honduras in 1956 can be considered latent manifestations of this same trend. Institutional upheavals in the armed-forces organization did not occur in Peru or Brazil, but even in these countries, the officer corps at least acquiesced in the rise of the political power of the labor-left—of APRA in Peru in 1945, and of Getúlio Vargas and the Labor Party (Partido Trabalhista Brasileiro, or PTB) in Brazil in 1950.

However, it was not long before the officer corps became increasingly disenchanted with the new labor-leftist leadership, both civilian and military. Things did not develop according to plan. In the military's eyes, these civilian politicos tended to be too radical, too doctrinaire, too demagogic. Their insistence upon overhasty implementation of agrarian-reform schemes, industrialization programs, and social-welfare measures in the face of growing resistance from traditionalist groups was leading, the military concluded, to social disintegration, political violence, and economic chaos. Rightist politicians went more and more frequently to plead with the military leaders to assume their responsibilities, once more, to save their countries.

The result was that even before the cycle of post-World War II popular revolution had run its course, it was overlapped by a new cycle of counterrevolution. The armed forces removed popularly elected Presidents and their labor-leftist party supporters in Ecuador in 1947, in Peru and Venezuela in 1948, in Brazil and Guatemala in 1954, and in Argentina in 1955. In every one of these countries, the successor civilian regimes to which the military ultimately transferred power were of a considerably more moderate stripe. This outcome was generally achieved by exiling the labor-leftist leaders and outlawing their party organizations.

And yet those forces that had the votes, the voices of change and reform, could not be kept down indefinitely. Two explosive new ingredients pumped into the Latin American political vortex gave the popular forces and their leaders new hope and encouragement. One was Castro's Cuba; the other was the Alliance for Progress. However, it was this combination of developments—the resurgence of labor-leftist forces, the revolutionary thrust of Castro's Cuba, and the implementation of the Alliance for Progress—that largely provoked the military to re-enter the political arena during the early 1960's.

Consider first Castro's Cuba. It is no accident that both of the Latin American nations that have steadfastly refused to sever relations with Cuba—Mexico and Uruguay—are nations in which the armed forces are, in large part, nonpolitical. In most states of Latin America, the military forced reluctant civilian governments to make a diplomatic break with Cuba. One does not have to seek far to understand the military's insistence on the break. The spectacle of Castro's utter destruction of Batista's armed forces and his summary execution of most of the senior officers in Cuba (more than 600 of them) filled the hearts of their professional brethren in the other countries of Latin America with horror and apprehension. They recall today that Castro started out as a moderate reformer but that he surprised nearly everyone

with the violence and extremism that characterized the immediate aftermath of his victory. As a result, the military in Latin
America today has come to suspect any popular reform movement as a potential threat to its own life and institutions.

A further cause for the military's apprehension over the future
of its own institution is the Alliance for Progress. To the military, the United States Government's public advocacy and support for crash programs of material development and social
change conducted through the medium of authentically democratic regimes is considered tantamount to encouraging political
instability and social disintegration.

The Intervention Process

The bugaboo of political instability and social disintegration
is promoted, of course, by the civilian minority determined to
resist government reform programs. Social groups whose properties and wealth are threatened by the proposed reforms—just
as large landholders and wealthy businessmen were by agrarian
and tax reforms—resort to almost any measure that will block the
government. In addition to utilizing the communications media
they control (the press, the radio, and the television stations), they
play upon the military's well-known fears of a violent social upheaval in order to save their own skins. This also is the method
of opposition political parties. They go to extraordinary lengths
to discredit the government. Sometimes they even encourage a
breakdown of law and order in an attempt to provoke military
intervention, but their more common tactic is to urge the military to do its duty and save the country from the irresponsible,
mob-backed government. Minority parties deliberately encourage
military intervention because this is the only way they can
achieve power. They do not want the armed forces to rule, except
for a very brief period, but merely to step in and impose sufficient
electoral restrictions upon the majority party to enable their
party to assume control of the government.

It is not always easy to determine, of course, to what degree military intervention is a cause, and to what degree it is merely an effect, of political instability. Certainly, the actions of the military cannot be understood adequately in isolation from the civilian pressures acting upon it. Generally speaking, except in the paradoxical case of Argentina, armed-forces leaders are inclined to exercise the most restraint in those countries where civilian political institutions are the most highly developed.

The actual decision to intervene, however, is made quite independently by military men themselves. Who are the decision-makers? They are, quite simply, the officers of senior rank in each of the armed services, the generals and the admirals in the various command posts. In some countries, as in Guatemala and Honduras, the colonels are in charge. Until such time as an officer reaches senior rank, he tends to eschew politics, and merely follows the orders of his superiors. However, when he reaches top rank, the armed forces' custodianship of the national interest inevitably involves him in political matters. The degree of influence a given general has depends upon the nature of his command. His opinions carry the greatest weight if he is Defense Minister. This Cabinet officer, although appointed by the President, is the armed-forces representative in the government, and therefore, his views represent the consensus of the various commanders of the armed services rather than those of the President. When military intervention takes place, it is usually the Defense or War Minister who orders the move against the President and assumes the office of Provisional President.

The decision-making process itself is quite simple. When a sufficient number of senior officers express doubts about a civilian government, all are summoned to their respective ministries to deliberate. Prior to each intervention, several meetings generally take place. A decision to take action does not come until such time as a consensus favors elimination of the civilian government. When that point is reached, only the execution of the coup itself remains.

And what is the political position of the decision-makers in today's armed forces? It is significant that they are products of the armed-forces institutional upheavals and popular revolutions that swept Latin America at the end of World War II. Then they were only junior officers, lieutenants and majors, but today, nearly a generation later, they are colonels and generals.

Because of their bitter experiences, already related, in the aftermath of those revolutions, they are not very sanguine about the prospects for viable democratic systems. They saw democracy tried recently, and they believe it has failed. They think that civilian political institutions are still too feeble, that the populace lacks political sophistication, and that, consequently, some system of guided or tutelary democracy will be necessary for an indefinite period. Also, for reasons of both personal and corporate self-interest, they are convinced that they cannot permit the return to power of the leaders and popular parties they initially cooperated with and then deposed, because they are apprehensive about the possibility of civilian vengeance.

The present military leaders' unwillingness to experiment with genuine democracy does not necessarily mean that they are agents of the oligarchy. Today's officers are lower-middle class in social origin,* but their institutional identification is so strong that it obliterates any meaningful identification with civilian social groups. Institutional considerations, the traditional insistence upon law and order, and the almost morbid fear of a social revolution that might destroy their organization combine in a political philosophy that is basically conservative. Today's military elite hews to no exotic foreign ideology. Rather, it merely responds to indigenous political conditions. It approves of reform but only at a pace moderate enough to avoid the threat of social disintegration and political chaos.

The Seven Coups Compared

Now, more specifically, why did the military make the actual decision to intervene? What does a comparative analysis of the

* Most Navy officers, however, tend to be middle to upper-middle class.

seven recent coups reveal? In all seven interventions, the armed forces sought to justify their actions before their own people and before the world as a necessary mission to save their respective nations from the menace of Communism and from ineffective civilian government. That is, they sought to justify the interventions in terms of the national interest. The Argentine armed forces charged that Frondizi was leading the nation down the road to Communism. Similar charges were leveled against Presidents Ydígoras in Guatemala, Arosemena in Ecuador, Bosch in the Dominican Republic, Villeda Morales in Honduras, and Goulart in Brazil.

These charges, however, have a kind of bogus quality. The proof of this was that the United States Government, just prior to the coups, was perfectly satisfied (except in the cases of Brazil and Ecuador) that policies of the civilian governments were anti-Communist and that the problem of combating Communism was being dealt with adequately by constitutional means. Since it is one of the main tasks of the United States diplomatic corps in Latin America to maintain a vigilant surveillance of the Communist threat, every embassy has a battery of experts, from the State Department, from the Central Intelligence Agency, and from the Pentagon, dealing with this problem on a day-to-day basis. Thus, it is most improbable that the United States is being fooled, or that it is blind to a menace that Latin America's armed forces see clearly.

The crux of the Communism issue here is semantic. A reasonably objective definition of Communism includes collectivization of the means of production, a dictatorship of the proletariat, and slavish adherence to the Chinese and/or Soviet foreign-policy lines—all of this to be accomplished through the agency of an authoritarian state under Communist Party domination. Not a single one of these characteristics seemed to be evident in any of these countries immediately prior to the coups, but one must appreciate the fact that an objective definition of Communism is considered woefully inadequate by the Latin American military. They believe that any kind of fundamental social-reform program might ultimately shade off into Communism, as it did in Cuba. In other words, the armed forces tend to equate the threat of Communism with any kind of program for accelerated social change and reform, and that is why many generals and admirals suspect Communist tendencies in those very political leaders whom Washington regards not only as stanchly anti-Communist, but also, as most likely to reduce the appeal of, and resist the growth of, Communism—men like Haya de la Torre in Peru, Betancourt in Venezuela, and Bosch in the Dominican Republic.

Prior to each of the coups, the military were egged on by civilians. The clamor against the governments they were about to depose was almost deafening. For example, military intervention was supported openly by the conservative press in Argentina, by the political right in Brazil, by the business community in Guatemala, by the landholders in Ecuador, by the rightist radio and television stations in the Dominican Republic, by the minority Nationalist Party in Honduras, and by Belaúnde Terry, who, after his defeat in the 1962 presidential election in Peru, stated: "Rather than see Haya get the presidency, I would have the military take power." If this kind of civilian urging did not actually swing the balance in behalf of pro-intervention officers, it almost certainly served to convince the military of the righteousness of their actions.

And what of the military's other rationalization for intervention—that they had to depose civilian governments because they had become inept, ineffective, and corrupt? This charge, upon close examination, also proves to be somewhat spurious. This becomes clear when it is noted that the governments that the military deposed were, for the most part, near the very end of their terms of office—less than ten days remained in Peru, less than three months in Honduras, and less than a year in Ecuador and Guatemala. Thus, it is hard to escape the conclusion that the coups, except in the Dominican Republic, were directed not against the incumbent governments but rather against their probable successors. In other words, these were preventive coups. In Brazil, also, the military intervention was undertaken to ensure against Goulart's extending his term of office.

Elections, either just completed or scheduled for the near future, triggered the coups. Since these interventions were designed either to nullify current election results or to stave off anticipated election outcomes, the military's actual motives become clear. Behind the ostensible reasons for intervening—the danger of Communism and the ineptness of incumbent governments—one finds the real reason is institutional self-interest. The military acted primarily to prevent the coming to power of civilian political groups they considered inimical to the interests of the armed forces. In Peru, they acted to protect themselves against possible vengeance from the *apristas,* whom they had ousted fourteen years earlier, and in Argentina, they intervened to guarantee themselves against retaliation from the *peronistas,* whom they had deposed seven years before. In Ecuador, they took action to prevent the return to power of Velasco Ibarra, the President they had ejected less than two years before; in Guatemala, the expected return of Arévalo to power made the military apprehensive of almost certain vengeance against the officers responsible for destroying the revolution he had launched in 1944; in Honduras, the armed forces acted to defend themselves against favored presidential candidate Rodas Alvarado, who openly courted the hated police and who threatened to bring an end to the military's traditional autonomy. And finally, in Brazil, the officer corps decided it could no longer tolerate a President who had undermined the discipline and morale of their institution. Thus was the corporate self-interest of the armed forces equated with the true national interest. Moreover, the veto of APRA in Peru, now a policy of more than thirty years' standing, and the continued veto against the *peronistas* in Argentina after nearly a decade suggest that the armed forces of Latin America today are an institution that neither forgives nor forgets easily.

As to the technique of intervention, every one was of the *coup d'état* (or *golpe de estado*) variety, that is, a concerted action of a unified military, as distinguished from the hitherto more frequent *cuartelazo* method, in which a barracks or interior garrison initiates action and calls upon the rest of the armed forces to join in the uprising. In all the 1962 and 1963 coups, the decision to intervene was made in the service ministries after a consensus to act had been arrived at, and thus there was no military resistance. The coups were all carefully prepared, then efficiently executed. They were all achieved within a very short time and with virtually no bloodshed.

In the wee hours of the morning, a detachment of troops, sometimes abetted by tanks, suddenly arrived at the executive residence and seized the President. At the same time, other troops seized control of the communications media—the telephone exchanges, the radio and television stations, and the progovernment presses. Meanwhile, firepower was concentrated at focal control points to meet any possible civilian resistance. At dawn came the *pronunciamiento,* the announcement by the armed forces to the people that they had assumed control of the government, that the constitution was now abrogated, and that the President and Congress were deposed. It was invariably explained that the armed forces were fulfilling their patriotic and constitutional duty to save the nation from the threat of Communism and the malevolence and ineptitude of the President and Congress. It was then announced that a junta, generally representing all the armed services, was in complete control and would rule until such time as the conditions that had obliged the military to intervene had been removed.

The aftermaths of the various coups were also roughly parallel. The military tracked down the Communists, exiled the leaders of the governments they deposed, and outlawed their parties. Thereupon, the junta called in an "independent" group of legal technicians to draft a new electoral statute, one that would guarantee against the return to power of the recently deposed elements. In Argentina within a year and a half, and in Peru within a year, elections were held and new governments installed, governments more acceptable to the wishes of the armed forces. This same process of preparation for a new kind of constitutional government was under way in Ecuador, Guatemala, Honduras, the Dominican Republic, and Brazil during 1964. All five countries had at least tentatively scheduled elections to be held by the end of 1965.

All the military interventions were proclaimed as distinctly temporary. Even if the armed forces were inclined to rule indefinitely, there were powerful pressures to prevent their doing so. Immediately upon assuming power, the juntas were urged by every remaining civilian political organization—especially by those which had encouraged the military to intervene in the first place—to restore constitutional procedures and civilian rule with a minimum of delay. In other words, the legitimacy of more than temporary military rule was immediately challenged by the entire civilian political sector, which understandably was impatient to get back in business as soon as possible. An added consideration was the military's incapacity for conducting the increasingly complex business of government. All the juntas, for example, found it necessary to call in civilian technicians to assume Cabinet posts and to draft the structural reforms preparatory to a return to constitutionalism. And in addition, foreign pressures were exerted, particularly by the United States, which demanded assurances of elections and reasonably early return to constitutional rule as the price of recognition and continuance of military- and economic-aid programs. Thus, in contrast to the past, a junta's *de facto* power and its guarantees to honor existing international obligations were insufficient to gain foreign approval and cooperation.

The Consequences of Intervention

Although the military interveners have now retired in two of the seven countries and are "making preparations" to do so in the other five, all seven interventions had profound political and social consequences upon the nations involved. One obvious political result is a blow against democracy, for in every case, the successor regime that emanated, or will emanate, from the junta rule is inevitably less representative than the government it deposed. Whatever has emerged, or may emerge, in the way of new elections, new constitutions, and new governments may be called democracy, but the military's veto against the return of the majority elements they ousted makes a mockery of that word. A likely secondary effect of the interventions will be future military interventions, for the interveners must now protect themselves against possible vengeance from resurgent democratic forces.

Even more serious are the social consequences. The seven coups meant something far more than the mere ouster of seven popularly elected Presidents. More fundamentally, they meant the strengthening of reaction. Even though the military did not act at the behest of the propertied elite, their actions, all the same, have had the effect of halting, or at least stalling, broad programs of social reform advocated by the governments they deposed, or by the governments they prevented from achieving power. Thus, it is the oligarchies that have reaped the benefits of the coups. This social consequence of military intervention raises one of the principal threats, both immediate and long range, to the whole Alliance for Progress program.

Was it possible to have avoided the crises between the governments and the armed forces that resulted in the coups? Probably not, nor have the determining conditions significantly changed today. On the one hand, there is the military's arrogation to itself of an inherent right to render judgments and exercise a veto power, if necessary, on civilian governments. Coupled with this institutional position above the law and the constitution is an armed-forces political consensus distinctly more conservative than that which prevails in the civilian sector. On the other hand, there are, or were, popularly based civilian governments elected upon the basis of promises of reform. To avoid a confrontation, either the armed forces or the civilian government must back down; the former are adamant in order to preserve their constitutional prerogatives, the latter in order to maintain its success as a political party. Both elements view compromise as a kind of suicide.

What inevitably happens is that when the military makes clear its determination to veto or water down a popular President's program for reform, that President, whose prime responsibility is to his constituents, attempts to maneuver his way out of the dilemma. Two courses lie open to him: either to try to break down the service resistance by subtle use of his promotion and appointment powers, as Frondizi, Prado, and Goulart hoped to do; or to try to develop a counterpoise to the armed forces in the form of a loyal police organization, as Villeda Morales attempted to do. Yet this dangerous game always leads ultimately to a clash, a clash in which the ballots of the President are utterly ineffectual against the bullets of the opposition generals. The attempt to use reason, to lecture the military on its responsibilities toward the law and the constitution does no good whatsoever, as Bosch discovered.

Although the military may have a clear conscience with respect to the patriotic motives for their intervention, the elements they deposed are not very charitable toward them. They see the coups as entirely unjustified, the products of a blind and exaggerated anti-Communism and of an absurd hypersensitivity to threats to the armed forces institution. They see the present military leaders as men who possess no appreciation of the urgent socio-economic problems their nations face. They see the armed forces as an institution devoid of any ideology whatsoever, impelled to action by a primitive, irascible patriotism and quick to veto any government, program, policy, party, or group they suspect might interfere with the selfish, vested interests of their sacred institution.

Furthermore, the civilian opposition by no means agrees that the military has any rights above the law; instead, they insist that the military appointed itself to a nation-saving mission without any popular mandate, that it has little or no true appreciation of national interest, and that it has no capacity for ruling, even for short periods of time. They see the military as the chief impediment to orderly resolution of their nation's social and economic problems. All these can be handled, the civilian opposition believes, by legal, constitutional means. However, when the military intervenes to prevent the democratic political resolution of differences that arise over economic and social problems, it interferes with the normal evolutionary process and thus only aggravates existing problems. They believe, in sum, that the political actions of the military serve only to disturb the political order without bringing any economic or social advantages.

But the military also has its civilian apologists—in the business community, in the professions, and among the landholders. Such men have generally become discouraged with all civilian political parties, both their leaders and their followers. They believe that an enforced order is essential to progress and that without military intervention disorder and chaos would prevail. They consider civilian parties incapable of running their countries and feel that their constant feuding and fractioning leads only to stalemate and drift. Consequently, the military has to occupy the power vacuum created, or else the nation will simply disintegrate. Such observers believe that military rule is an inevitable result of Latin America's political immaturity.

In rejoinder, the partisans of democratic processes argue that it is the military itself, through its constant interference, that is largely responsible for the area's lack of political progress. The real problem, they contend, is that the military's firepower is so overwhelming that no conceivable civilian demand for constitutional rule can possibly overcome it. Even so, it is pointed out, an extraordinarily large percentage of the eligible voters participate in all free elections. And as to the military's alleged capabilities for governing, they challenge armed-forces supporters to name a single military regime in Latin America that has either elevated living standards or made significant headway toward solving its problems.

According to a more pessimistic view, the armed forces are but one sick segment of a generally corrupt Latin American body politic, which includes factious political parties, opportunistic leaders, a myopic oligarchy, and misguided nationalists and extremists both on the left and on the right. If this view is valid, the military deserve no more than a share of the blame for Latin America's current political malaise.

7. Kennedy and the Latin American Generals

Encouragement of Democracy

The Administration of President John F. Kennedy made some truly fundamental alterations in the traditional United States policies toward Latin American military rulers. The Eisenhower Administration, in its aid and assistance programs, made little distinction between dictatorial and democratic governments. It accepted all *de facto* regimes, regardless of how they achieved power, so long as they were anti-Communist and friendly toward the United States. It went so far as to collaborate openly with General Perón in Argentina and even to grant Legion of Merit citations to Generals Pérez Jiménez of Venezuela and Odría of Peru.* The operative premise seemed to be that dictators offered the surest defense against the threat of Communism.

This pragmatic approach to Latin America's internal political problems was rejected by Kennedy, who substituted definite notions and policy actions in behalf of democratic idealism. During the presidential campaign, he had been sharply critical of too close United States identification with unrepresentative regimes. The first concrete evidence of an actual policy change occurred on February 15, 1961, when the three-week-old Administration exacted from the new junta in El Salvador, as a condition of recognition, promises of early elections and a speedy return to constitutional government.

* The bitter rewards of these policies were reaped in Vice-President Nixon's ill-fated 1958 tour of Latin America.

A key feature of the President's March 31, 1961, Alliance for Progress speech was his plea for democracy. He clearly indicated his disapproval of irresponsible and predatory militarism in Latin America and called for political freedom and the elimination of tyranny. The democratic process, in the President's eyes, was a *sine qua non* for social revolution by evolutionary, rather than violent, means.

The President seized the opportunity to implement his democratic principles in the political crisis that erupted in the Dominican Republic following the May, 1961, assassination of dictator Rafael Trujillo. Diplomatic pressure was applied to prevent the retention of power by the dictator's heirs; when this proved insufficient, a Navy task force was stationed offshore, with Marines ready to land, just to make the point against the Trujillos, and in behalf of democracy, unmistakably clear. Thus, largely as a result of United States coercion, free elections were held a year later, and democracy came, though for but a short time, to the Dominican Republic.

March 29, 1962, marked the Kennedy Administration's first confrontation with a military coup against a freely elected, constitutional government—in Argentina. When the coup appeared imminent, United States diplomats were instructed to spare no efforts in trying to head it off by warning the Argentine generals and admirals that such action would conflict with the Alliance for Progress's objectives in regard to political freedom. When this had no effect and President Frondizi was ousted, Washington then seriously considered withholding recognition and cutting off all aid. However, it finally conceded the military's point that no interruption of constitutional processes had really occurred since Senate President José María Guido, the constitutional successor to Frondizi, was immediately sworn in as President. Thus, the question of recognition was not even officially raised, and there was no interruption in either the military- or economic-aid programs. But the Kennedy Administration soon discovered it had been duped. For not only did Guido become a mere puppet of the ruling military, but also, Congress was prohibited from meeting. The fact of actual rule by generals and admirals was revealed to all because of the transparency of the constitutional façade.

The next test for democracy came three months later, in Peru. Prior to the June 10 presidential elections, the military hierarchy had given ample indication that they might seize power if Haya de la Torre emerged victorious. This brought repeated warnings from James Loeb, United States Ambassador in Lima, that Washington would surely refuse to recognize a regime emanating from a military coup. When the elections resulted in a plurality for Haya and the military appeared on the verge of taking over the government, Senator Hubert Humphrey cautioned that such action would mean the end of United States aid to Peru. Armed-forces leaders were unimpressed; these same threats had been issued in Buenos Aires three months before and had, at that time, proved to be empty. Accordingly, on July 18, 1962, the coup was carried out, and a junta was set up to rule.

This time the reaction from Washington was prompt and clearcut. The Administration suspended diplomatic relations, stopped the military-assistance program, and cut off all economic aid going to Peru under the Alliance for Progress. Here, there was no doubt that democratic principles were involved, but the larger Latin American nations, particularly Mexico, appeared to question whether the United States had the right to assume the role of policeman for democracy in Latin America. Thus, when the major Latin American and European nations, as well, recognized the junta—Argentina was the first to extend recognition—Kennedy's policy of international ostracism of the new Peruvian regime broke down. With almost no diplomatic support, except for several of the smaller Latin American nations, under pressure from United States business interests in Peru and from the Peruvian populace (two-thirds of whom had supported presidential candidates other than Haya de la Torre), the United States on August 17 recognized Peru and restored economic aid and, a short time later, resumed military assistance. As a face-saving condition for recognition and aid, Washington did succeed in getting a promise from the junta to hold elections within a reasonable length of time and, in the interim, to work for the economic and social progress of the Peruvian people.

The favorable diplomatic denouements obtained by the *golpistas* (coup leaders) in Argentina and Peru were interpreted as a green light from Washington for the military elsewhere in Latin America to right situations of civilian misrule. Accordingly, the year 1963 was an open season for bagging constitutional governments. The formula for dealing with protests from Washington had been provided: Rationalize the coups by charges of Communist infiltration and gross misgovernment; follow this by promises to hold elections and restore constitutional processes within a "reasonable" length of time. This was the technique used by the juntas in Guatemala, Ecuador, the Dominican Republic, and Honduras. It worked in the first two countries; in the latter two, the officers ran into serious, though only temporary, difficulties.

In Guatemala, the colonels took over the government on March 31, 1963, with an air of great confidence. They, too, had received warnings from United States diplomats that their planned seizure of power would be construed as direct opposition to United States policies in behalf of democracy. However, they knew that Washington had long been disenchanted with the inept, unprogressive, and corrupt government of President Ydígoras, and they were certain that the Kennedy Administration was having nightmares over the very real prospect that Juan Arévalo, considered extremely hostile to the United States, would succeed to the presidency if the elections were carried out. Accordingly, the colonels calculated that Washington would be willing to compromise its principles of democratic idealism in order to get rid of two men, Ydígoras and Arévalo, considered a menace to its security interests in Central America. The colonels calculated correctly. They received recognition and continued military and economic support from the United States on April 18, less than three weeks following the coup, in exchange for nothing more than a vague promise to conduct elections, perhaps sometime in 1965.

Similar were the calculations of the Ecuadorian military as they planned their coup. They knew Washington was unhappy with President Arosemena for many reasons: He had refused to break relations with Cuba, he had allowed Communists to infiltrate the bureaucracy, he imbibed excessively, and he had been unable to promote economic or social progress. His public condemnation of United States policy, while in a state of inebriation and with Ambassador Maurice Birnbaum present, provided the military with the ideal opportunity to take an action that Washington, they believed, would certainly not condemn. They were right. This time the Kennedy Administration sacrificed its democratic principles completely in order to get rid of a constitutional government it considered inimical to its best interests. In fact, when the coup occurred, the customary protest in behalf of political freedom and democracy was not even made. Rather, Ambassador Birnbaum indicated the coup was probably a good thing, and State Department officials echoed his sentiments. The junta was praised for its "sense of mission" and its progressive outlook, and in less than three weeks, recognition came in exchange for assurances that elections would be held within a "reasonable" length of time. The military- and economic-aid programs were not even interrupted.

Less than two months later, the military in the Dominican Republic prepared to depose President Juan Bosch. Here the generals were hardly impressed when Ambassador John B. Martin cautioned them that a coup against a government so strongly supported by the State Department would bring sharp reactions from Washington. More important were their impressions from the United States military personnel, the Military Advisory Assistance Group (MAAG) and the Army Mission officers, some of whom reportedly agreed with them that Bosch was probably a

Communist.* Certainly, the generals reasoned, the Pentagon would applaud their seizure of power. However, just a few hours after the September 26 *coup d'état,* the Kennedy Administration suspended relations and cut off all aid programs. The State Department publicly condemned the military action and announced that "any overthrow of a democratically elected government is a loss to the policies of the countries of the hemisphere, including our own." It had apparently not felt this way in the cases of Guatemala or Ecuador. Thus, Washington seemed to be saying that it supported democracy, but with certain qualifications. The democratic government in question, it seemed, also had to be the kind of government Washington approved of, that is, responsible, effective, and anti-Communist.

Within a week of the Dominican coup, the Honduran military threatened a similar action. The Kennedy Administration employed everything short of armed intervention to head it off. Ambassador Charles Burrows repeatedly warned Colonel Oswaldo López, the armed-forces chief, that Washington would react strongly to a military power seizure, and to make his point unmistakably clear, he had his MAAG and Mission officers also caution López. A United States major general was dispatched to issue similar warnings. Through October 2, López denied that a coup was contemplated; on October 3, he carried it out.

This was the last straw. That very day, the United States not only suspended diplomatic ties and all aid programs, but announced that it was withdrawing all its aid personnel, both military and civilian, from Honduras and the Dominican Republic and assigning them elsewhere. Secretary of State Dean Rusk explained: "Under existing conditions in Honduras and the Dominican Republic, there is no opportunity for effective collaboration by the United States under the Alliance for Progress." This action was stern warning to the military in all Latin America that the United States would no longer cooperate with governments that came to power by use of force. Vague promises of an

* See *The New York Times,* October 5, 1963.

ultimate return to constitutionalism would no longer be sufficient to get support.

Colonel López in Honduras and his uniformed colleagues in the Dominican Republic were furious. They argued that they were the objects of discrimination. Their actions, they maintained, sprang from the same patriotic, anti-Communist, motives as those of their brethren in Ecuador and Guatemala, and yet the latter received United States recognition, aid, and support while Honduras and the Dominican Republic did not. Why? United States diplomats could explain only that Washington had now decided that militarism in Latin America had gone too far, that it considered coups serious threats to the whole Alliance for Progress program, and that henceforth it was going to stand firmly behind the principles of political freedom and democracy for Latin America.

And it is true that although President Kennedy wavered a bit and bowed to expediency in the Guatemalan and Ecuadorian cases, he now returned unmistakably to the fundamentals of democratic idealism espoused when he took office. On November 18, 1963, just four days before his tragic death, he reiterated his idealistic political policies and beliefs before the Inter-American Press Association in Miami in these unequivocal terms:

> Political democracy and stability . . . is at the core of our hopes for the future.
>
> There can be no progress if people have no faith in tomorrow. That faith is undermined when men seek the reins of power, ignoring the restraints of constitutional procedures. They may even do so out of a sincere desire to benefit their own country. But democratic government demands that those in opposition accept the defeats of today and work toward remedying them within the machinery of peaceful change. Otherwise, in return for momentary satisfaction, we tear apart the fabric and the hope of lasting democracy.
>
> Whatever may be the case in other parts of the world, this is a hemisphere of free men capable of self-government. It is in accordance with this belief that the United States will continue to support the efforts of those seeking to establish and maintain constitutional democracy.

As United States diplomatic and economic pressures did little to deter military men from seizing power once they had made up their minds to do so, the Kennedy Administration began to show increasing sympathy to a hemisphere-wide approach to the problem. Venezuela and Costa Rica were the leaders in a move for collective action in defense of constitutional government. Following the Peruvian coup of July, 1962, they called for an OAS meeting to consider the crisis, but only the Honduran and Dominican governments, soon to fall victim to military coups themselves, supported the move. Resisting it, and hewing to the traditional Latin American doctrine of nonintervention, were the organization's three largest nations—Brazil, Mexico, and Argentina. The Guatemalan coup of March, 1963, brought warning by the United States that traditional Latin American attitudes against intervention might well be preventing collective action in behalf of democracy. Venezuela tried again to get OAS action on the problem in July, but still only six countries (Colombia, El Salvador, and the original four) were willing to consider it. The United States abstained from voting pending crystallization of a more positive Latin American attitude. Then came the Dominican and Honduran coups, and finally, in November, 1963, the Venezuelan Government's third call for collective action in defense of democracy was supported 18 to 1, Guatemala casting the only negative vote. An OAS Consultative Meeting of Foreign Ministers to consider methods for strengthening democracy in Latin America was scheduled for early 1964.*

The Cuban Question

Although the Alliance for Progress program was designed to head off new Castro-type upheavals, the problem of Cuba itself remained, and in dealing with it, the Kennedy Administration sought the cooperation of Latin America's armed forces. Re-

* For reasons not entirely clear, such a meeting was never held, but certainly the shift in United States policy following the assassination of President Kennedy (see Chapter 9) was a factor.

peatedly the Eisenhower Administration had tried to interest the
Latin American military in some kind of joint venture designed
to bring the Communist threat in Cuba to an end. Yet despite the
fact that all Latin American nations had signed the 1947 Inter-
American Treaty of Reciprocal Assistance, under which they
agreed to take collective measures to repel external aggression in
the Western hemisphere, despite the fact that the Pentagon continued to sell arms at bargain prices to all the countries (save
Cuba) in order that they might cooperate in the defense of the
hemisphere, and despite the fact that eleven nations received
military-aid grants under the Mutual Security Act for the purpose
of participating in collective defense against the Communist
threat to the hemisphere, Latin America's armed forces showed
no willingness to do any fighting outside their own borders.

As the inter-American security system was able to produce
nothing in the way of effective collective action to preserve
hemisphere security, and as concern over a Soviet-armed, Com-
munist-controlled Cuba mounted, the patience of the United
States gave out, and it was decided to go it alone. Carrying
through preparations begun under Eisenhower, the Kennedy
Administration attempted in April of 1961 to carry out a policy
that can be described only as unilateral, indirect intervention in
Cuba—that is, arming, training, and transporting an invasion
force made up of Cuban exiles. The result was a fiasco; the 1,500
invaders proved no match for Castro's 300,000 troops.

Unwilling, for many reasons, to consider using United States
personnel in a full-scale military assault upon Cuba, Washington
attempted once more to get collective action against the Castro
regime. The aim at the Eighth Consultative Meeting of Foreign
Ministers, in Punta del Este, Uruguay, in January, 1962, was to
isolate Cuba diplomatically. In attempting to achieve this, the
Kennedy Administration not only exerted tremendous pressure
upon the civilian governments of Ecuador, Argentina, Brazil,
Chile, Bolivia, Uruguay, and Mexico to sever relations with the
Castro regime, but also encouraged the military sectors of the
reluctant civilian regimes to do their part to promote the United

States anti-Castro policy. At Punta del Este, the Argentine and Ecuadorian governments were able to resist Washington's pressures, but they were subsequently unable to resist those of their own armed forces, which within four months forced both Presidents Frondizi and Arosemena to accept the United States position. At least partly because of United States pressures, the Brazilian military kept a short halter upon President Goulart with respect to his pro-Cuban policy, although it could not force him to break relations.

Also at Punta del Este, at the urging of the United States, an Inter-American Security Committee, manned by five high-ranking officers, was established to make recommendations for fighting Communist subversion in the Western hemisphere. The committee's main job was to deal with the revolutionary threat emanating from Castro's Cuba.

However, before the year 1962 was out, the Kennedy Administration had to deal with a genuine and immediate military threat from Cuba, for in July of 1962, Russia decided not only to shore up the Castro regime economically, but also to make use of it in the Cold War against the United States. The Soviets sent in thousands of troops, advisers, and technicians, plus transports laden with war materials. When the Kennedy Administration discovered offensive weaponry in the form of Soviet jet bombers and missiles, it promptly declared, on October 22, 1962, a quarantine on shipment of all such weapons into Cuba and proposed a naval blockade to stop it.

The following morning, Secretary of State Dean Rusk put forward a resolution before an emergency session of the OAS Council authorizing the use of force to guarantee compliance with the blockade. It was approved unanimously. To help enforce the blockade, nine Latin American nations made cooperative gestures: Argentina offered two destroyers; Honduras and Peru offered troops; Costa Rica, Nicaragua, Panama, the Dominican Republic, Guatemala, and Venezuela offered temporary use of their bases. This was the greatest display of collective willingness to help defend the hemisphere in the entire history of the OAS.

How much cooperation Latin America would actually furnish
was never put to the test, for the military crisis was averted by
Russia's decision not to run the blockade, and by her subsequent
removal of offensive weapons and combat personnel from Cuba
during the remainder of 1962, 1963, and 1964.

Counterinsurgency

Even before the actual military threat from Cuba had been
removed, the Kennedy Administration had rejected the heretofore prevailing United States military policies designed to promote hemisphere defense against external aggression. This "new
look" involved several reassessments. Not only was invasion of
Latin America from abroad now considered a most unlikely
eventuality, but the whole concept of meaningful collective defense was viewed as a myth. In addition, Washington concluded
that not only were the Latin American military generally unwilling to lend assistance outside their own borders, but also their
armed-forces organizations were too weak to be of use in meeting
any major external threat.

The Cuban experience—that is, Castro's successful guerrilla
operation against the Batista regime, which had been advised by
the United States military missions and had been granted substantial military aid under a Mutual Defense Assistance Pact—
and the evidence of Sino-Soviet world-wide subversion tactics
soon gave rise in the Kennedy Administration to discussions on
how to combat future Communist and proto-Communist guerrilla operations in Latin America. During 1961, the decision was
made to shift the basis for military aid to Latin America from
hemisphere defense to internal security, from protection of the
coasts to internal defense of Latin American governments against
Castro-Communist guerrilla warfare.

The new counterinsurgency program for Latin America was
launched during 1962 by expanding the United States Army's
Special Forces, which had already proved valuable in the fighting
in Southeast Asia. The United States Caribbean Command, with

headquarters in the Canal Zone, began putting its strategic emphasis upon counterrevolutionary tactics, and Latin American officers were selected for antiguerrilla training at the Army's Special Forces School at Fort Bragg, North Carolina, and at its Jungle Warfare School at Fort Girlick in the Canal Zone. In addition, United States antiguerrilla advisory teams gave instruction to armies throughout Latin America. The armed forces were encouraged to equip themselves in the future with jeeps, helicopters, grenades, and carbines rather than jets, tanks, and carriers, which had no relevance whatever to the problems at hand.

An integral part of the counterinsurgency program was "civic action." That is, Latin America's armed forces were encouraged to contribute their special skills and resources to help resolve some of the economic and social problems of the civilian sector. This involved such projects as the building of feeder roads, the purification of water supplies, the construction of schools and irrigation facilities, and the lending of assistance in health and sanitation programs.

The basic motive behind civic action also emanated from the Cuban experience, where guerrilla successes were very largely a consequence of the Cuban people's hatred of their Army. The Kennedy Administration realized that the armed forces in many Latin American countries, largely because of the predatory militarism of the past, had become dangerously isolated from the civilian populations. The hope was that through civic-action programs, they would be able to regain and hold the respect of the people. If they succeeded in doing so, it was assumed that the people would then cooperate with the soldiers in antiguerrilla operations, rather than support the guerrillas, as they did in Cuba.

The army antiguerrilla programs and the civic-action programs were both designed to deal with possible trouble in rural areas, but the Kennedy Administration did not ignore the equally important, if not more important, problem of Castro-Communist rioting and terrorism in the cities. To deal with it, the Agency for

International Development established, in July, 1962, an Inter-
American Policy Academy at Fort Davis in the Canal Zone. Here,
during the remainder of 1962 and in 1963, more than 600 policemen from fifteen Latin American countries were trained to
handle mob demonstrations and to do counterintelligence work.
In addition, special police-training programs were set up in
twelve Latin American countries. One line of reasoning behind
the police-training programs was that if the police could maintain law and order in the capital cities, the armed forces might be
less inclined to seize power from the civilian authorities.

An additional aspect of the Kennedy Administration's counterinsurgency program was its effort to curtail the training of
guerrillas and subversives in Cuba, as well as the flow of arms
and propaganda from the island. To these ends, it worked
through the Inter-American Security Committee. The Committee
estimated that Cuba was training annually 1,000 to 1,500 Communist agents from other Latin American countries in assorted
types of sabotage, terrorist, riot-promotion, and guerrilla techniques. It prepared a report, adopted by the OAS Council in
April, 1963, asking all the governments of Latin America to
adopt rigid passport regulations on travel to Cuba and to exercise
greater surveillance over the traffic in Cuban arms and propaganda. In November, 1963, a three-ton cache of small arms of
Cuban origin was seized by Venezuelan authorities. An OAS Foreign Ministers' meeting set up to deal with this problem in July,
1964, voted fifteen to four to impose mandatory diplomatic and
economic sanctions against Castro's Cuba.*

A Policy Critique

However enthusiastic Kennedy's New Frontiersmen were in
behalf of counterinsurgency and however methodical they were
in arranging for implementation of the program, they did not
convince the Latin American military leaders that this was the

* Bolivia, Chile, Mexico, and Uruguay voted against taking such action, but
Chile and Bolivia subsequently did break off diplomatic relations with Cuba.

best way to fight Communism. The Administration's thesis that Castro's success was due to guerrilla-warfare techniques, unbeatable by the use of conventional armies, was not accepted. Instead, the Latin American generals and admirals maintained that Castro had won because Batista's armed forces were weak and ill-equipped. Accordingly, they demanded tremendous amounts of new equipment—tanks, jets, destroyers—to defend their own countries. The military, particularly those of Brazil and Venezuela, took advantage of the October, 1962, missile crisis to double and triple their demands for heavy military hardware to defend against possible invasion.

Latin America's armed forces were willing to cooperate with the United States antiguerrilla-training missions and to devote a unit or two of their establishments to antiguerrilla-warfare operations, but they were unwilling to make the kind of major shift in emphasis encouraged by Washington. For example, in the $76-million annual United States military-aid programs for Latin America for 1962 and 1963, the equipment sent continued to be overwhelmingly of the heavy conventional hardware variety. More than two-thirds of the aid for air forces, for example, went for jets.

Then, too, the counterinsurgency units did not always perform as intended. In Peru, the antiguerrilla commandos spearheaded the ouster of President Manuel Prado. In the Dominican Republic, the United States-trained police joined the Army in ousting President Bosch, following which both the police and the anti-guerrilla units, trained during 1963 by a forty-four-man United States Army Mission, were used to hunt down Bosch's non-Communist partisans in the name of anti-Communism. In Guatemala and Ecuador, too, there was every indication that the counter-insurgency forces, both the police and Army units, were being used principally to stifle the political thrust of the non-Communist left. In Honduras, the police, trained for counterinsurgency, got into a dispute with the Army that resulted in the elimination of the police and the assumption of their functions by the Army.

Largely because of the military assaults upon constitutional
governments, the whole Latin American military policy of the
Kennedy Administration came under increasing criticism from
the United States Congress, particularly from the Senate, where
the feeling seemed to be growing that the Administration's military policies were defeating its political aims. Following the
Argentine coup, Senator Frank Carlson (Republican, Kansas)
demanded the elimination of the military aid. Following the
coup in Peru, Senator Ernest Gruening (Democrat, Alaska) made
similar demands. He saw the coups as by-products of military-aid
programs that had failed both in their military objective of bolster-
ing hemisphere defense and in their political objective of exerting
a democratic influence upon the Latin American officer corps.
The coups in the Dominican Republic and Honduras produced
a proposal by Senator Wayne Morse (Democrat, Oregon) that
all aid to regimes ruled by the military in Latin America be cut
off. In the foreign-aid bill for fiscal 1964, Morse introduced an
amendment reducing military aid to Latin America by 15 per
cent, but in the final bill, the President was granted authority to
continue the programs at the customary $76-million level if he
decided it would be in the national interest.

Certainly, an argument could be made that the various policy
goals of the Kennedy Administration were coming into conflict,
and that the chief reason for this was Washington's ineffectiveness
in exercising control over the actions of Latin America's military
organizations. Though the Administration rejected hemisphere defense as a military concept, it continued, for the purpose of keeping
the politically powerful armed forces friendly, a substantial aid
program and sales of arms at bargain prices, only to witness the repeated use of such arms for internecine warfare among the various services and for assaults upon constitutional governments. It
launched a special program to deal with Castro-Communist insurgency, only to see the wielders of the weapons use them against
the non-Communist left, which Washington believed to be the
best defense against Communism.

The most unexpected and unintended repercussion of all was that military assistance was contributing new political strength to an antireform institution—the role assumed by the armed forces themselves—just when Washington had hoped to carry out a broad-scale program of economic and social change through democratic constitutional governments. By force of arms, six such governments were destroyed during Kennedy's term of office.

The Administration's policies were not always consistent. Its general policy was to encourage the growth of responsible apolitical military organizations so that democracy might have a better chance to function; yet, when it wanted to isolate Cuba, it did not hesitate to make political use of the military against policies of the civilian governments of Argentina and Ecuador. Also, it compromised democratic principles for the sake of expediency in accepting the coups in Guatemala and Ecuador. Finally, it began to veer toward a watered-down definition of democracy by going along with vetoes issued by the military against majority-supported civilian politicians.

The military programs also came under increasingly severe criticism from Latin American civilian parties. Whether or not it was United States aid that had swung the balance in behalf of military intervention, they could not help noting that United States-manufactured tanks and jets were the weapons of the coups and that United States-trained officers were the perpetrators of the coups. In Honduras, for example, the infantry and air-force battalions especially developed for defense-of-the-hemisphere missions were the ones used to topple the Villeda Morales government.

As military intervention in many countries blocked democratic social revolution, it gave added weight to Castro's oft-repeated assertion that there is no alternative between violent social upheavals and military dictatorship. And it was certainly true that, despite its noble efforts and intentions, the Kennedy Administration accomplished little in furthering the cause of democracy in Latin America.

8. Prospects

Conservatism of the Contemporary Military Leaders

When the Latin American political spectrum is considered as a unit, there is little question that the armed forces are a conservative, antirevolutionary institution standing in the way of the achievement of evolutionary social revolution by democratic means. During the early 1960's, the armed forces intervened in Argentina, Brazil, Peru, Guatemala, Ecuador, the Dominican Republic, and Honduras—which contain over half the area's total population—to depose or restrain reform-minded civilian political leaders and groups, or to prevent their coming to power. In three other countries (Paraguay, Haiti,* and Nicaragua), armed might is used to maintain traditional, essentially reactionary, dictatorships. Thus, ten of Latin America's twenty republics are gripped in military vises designed to hold back the pressures of social revolution.

In Mexico, Bolivia, Uruguay, Costa Rica, Colombia, Chile, and Panama, which together account for a little more than a third of Latin America's land area and population, the armed forces have thus far assumed an apolitical posture in the face of the new revolutionary pressures resulting from Castro's Cuba and Alliance for Progress programs. Only in Uruguay, however, have the armed forces stood aside while the civilian leaders moderated

* President François Duvalier maintains his tyranny in Haiti through the Tontons-Macoutes, a 5,000-man secret-police organization. The latter are opposed by the regular armed forces, the Garde d'Haiti, but the dictator has rendered the Garde an inferior force by confiscating most of its arms.

their country's social problems by constitutional means. In three of these countries, violent upheavals occurred (in Mexico in 1910, in Costa Rica in 1948, and in Bolivia in 1952), and during this process, the regular armed forces were destroyed and replaced by revolutionary armies, which are today under the control of the civilian authorities.

In Chile, Colombia, and Panama, the armed forces have had little motive, thus far, to intervene in the growing socio-political crisis, for in all three countries, conservative elements have been able to maintain control through the democratic, constitutional structure. But the fact remains that what exists in Chile, Colombia, and Panama today is a species of classical Greek democracy, with the exclusiveness and static quality that implies.

In none of the three has there been any meaningful social reform as yet, even though the pressures for such reform are near the breaking point. Should the variously fragmented, shattered, and disorganized labor-leftist majority elements in these countries ever be able to combine or rebuild for an electoral victory, the present apolitical stance of the armed forces might be seriously shaken. The test could come in Chile during 1965 if, as seems likely, either the candidate of the Popular Action Front (Frente de Acción Popular, or FAP) or the Christian Democrats should succeed in winning the September, 1964, presidential election. Panama had a military ruler as recently as 1955, and Colombia as recently as 1957, and the prospects are that the military will return to attempt to moderate the intensifying social crisis in both countries in the years ahead.

Only in Peru, Venezuela, and El Salvador, which contain 10 per cent of Latin America's total population, are the armed forces today defending representative, popularly elected governments devoted to sound programs of political, social, and economic progress. Yet all three of these democracies are fragile experiments, and it is far from certain that Presidents Belaúnde in Peru, Leoni in Venezuela, and Rivera in El Salvador will serve out their terms without military intervention.

In Peru, Belaúnde's democratic image is somewhat tarnished by the circumstances of his election. However, his government appears determined to promote social change and reform. But it still remains doubtful whether meaningful implementation of reform programs within a democratic framework is possible in the face of the resistance, heretofore always effective, of the landed and business oligarchies.

Similarly, in El Salvador, a popular, democratic, reform-oriented government is in power, but President Rivera must overcome not only the resistance of the powerful landholding clique, but also the Castro-Communists. His Administration's capacity for maintaining law and order will determine whether democracy and social progress will prevail or whether a new military intervention will bring them to a halt.

In Venezuela, Betancourt's unprecedented achievement of serving out his full term of office in a country hitherto dominated by military dictators is indeed a promising omen for the future of democracy. However, the officer corps is more conservative than his successor's left-of-center government. If the determined Castro-Communists succeed in creating chaos by terrorism and subversion, the military may well attempt to resume its accustomed governing role.

Finally, there is Cuba, where a revolutionary army, having destroyed the regulars in the name of democracy, has been turned into a vehicle for authoritarian Communism. This resulted from the perversion of the revolution by Major Fidel Castro and his subsequent conversion to Communism. Today, the whole armed-forces organization is provided with pro-Communist leadership. At the pinnacle of the military pyramid, directly under Fidel, is Major Raúl Castro, with the lines of political power descending through other majors serving as governors in the provinces, and captains and lieutenants filling posts at the district and municipal levels.

Castro's whole military organization is equipped with modern arms and has been trained by Soviet military technicians. From the standpoint of both modern equipment and size (200,000 regulars plus 100,000 militiamen), the Cuban Army is probably the most powerful in Latin America. Yet because of the United States, it constitutes no direct military threat to any Latin American country. What is significant is its overwhelming power on the island. Its equipment and size make Cuba's military organization more secure against possible resistance from its own people than any other armed-forces organization in Latin America. It guarantees Castro the capability to carry out his Communist experiment at home, to promote the export of his system to the rest of Latin America, and to defend himself against any conceivable attack that might come from Latin America.

Castro-Communism, Militarism, and Democracy

In the realm of social revolution in Latin America today, there are three major political forces at work. The tocsin for social reform is rung loudest by the Communist parties. Abetted by propaganda and financial, moral, and arms support from Cuba, Russia, and China, the local Communists are conniving with the extreme leftists in all Latin American countries to get on with the business of social revolution immediately.

The Sino-Soviet split is reflected in Latin America by disagreement over technique: Russia favors a drive for power by interim cooperation, under existing political and legal systems, with other leftist political organizations; China advocates incitement of class warfare to produce immediate violent social upheaval. Castro's Cuba, though shored up materially by Russia, is ideologically closer to the Chinese line, perhaps largely as a result of Cuba's own recent Chinese-style revolution. Although the Sino-Soviet schism has split Communist parties in several Latin American countries, it is decidedly the "revolution now" advocates who have the upper hand. They have stirred the minds of Latin America's youth and caused many to lose faith in democracy. They argue that all Latin American democracies are pseudo democracies, mere façades behind which Yankee imperialism and the domestic oligarchies try to hide. They proclaim that there is no genuine democratic alternative to either violent social upheaval or rightist military dictatorship, and consider their view vindicated by the coups of 1962, 1963, and 1964. They are trying to provoke military intervention wherever democracy attempts to take hold. They believe that with military dictatorship, their prospects for arousing a violent social upheaval are best.

This Castro-Communist challenge is a formidable one in Latin America today. And if Russia continues to back Castro, it is likely to continue for several reasons. First of all, there is the inspiration of Castro's Cuba itself. The revolutionary regime is now in its sixth year, and there appears little immediate prospect, despite many internal economic weaknesses, that the regime will collapse soon. Second, there is little likelihood that the rest of the hemisphere can, or is willing to, destroy it. Finally, there is good reason to assume that Castro's ardor for exporting his revolution to the rest of Latin America will continue. For he sees his mission today in messianic, Bolivarian terms; he believes himself destined to extend his Sierra Maestra triumph to the Andes. And continuing to give weight to his arguments, and to win him adherents, is the growing number of military seizures of power and, as a consequence, the apparently repeated failures of democracy.

Yet, despite its recent setbacks, democracy still has the overwhelming support of Latin America's people. Democracy, too, is abetted by foreign support, mainly from the United States, of the propaganda, financial, moral, and military varieties. Democracy, too, like Communism, preaches social revolution, but by evolutionary means, within the law and under a constitutional system. It is true that many civilian political organizations operating inside the democratic system in Latin America are quite opposed to the concept of social revolutions, but in free elections they cannot win. Governments resistant to social reform can achieve power constitutionally only where the democratic left is fragmented (as in Chile) or is unable to organize (as in Colombia).

Where there is a clear and free choice, the democratic left wins over the extreme left and the right. In some cases, notably Venezuela and Peru, right-of-center parties have so little appeal that they have disappeared entirely.

And yet, democracy has been receding at an alarming rate since 1961, and the prospects are that it will probably recede even further before it begins to recover ground. This is likely because genuine democratic governments are also governments that promote social change and reform. As attempts to restructure outmoded societies continue, the oligarchies are going to continue to resist—within the law, if possible, but outside it, if necessary. Although the oligarchies are finding it increasingly difficult to convince the armed forces that they have an identity of interests, they still have the power to provoke military intervention by discrediting democratic government through their communications media, by refusing to cooperate economically or politically, and by inciting violence and a general breakdown of law and order.

In addition, the armed forces have their own reasons for opposition to democracy and social change in any form. It is not that the armed forces are opposed to social change *per se,* but rather, that they feel the process of social change disturbs law and order, and threatens the welfare and interests of the nation along with those of the armed forces.

Thus far in the early 1960's, the military has been either unwilling or unable to distinguish between democratic and Communist reform elements. Its mood has been one of blind, exaggerated anti-Communism. Militarism in Latin America today, in contrast to both Communism and democracy, is a political force that, on balance, brings social change and reform programs to a halt. It does not, therefore, constitute an alternative choice in the process of social revolution; it merely holds up that revolution.

The hierarchy in the officer corps seems to have lost contact with the political and social realities in its respective nations. It appears to possess no ideology whatsoever, only a negative reaction to all programs and persons who advocate what is in its view too rapid a change. What is more, the military's panic in the face of growing pressures for social revolution in Latin America is contagious. It has spread from southeastern South America to the Andes, to Central America, and into the Caribbean, and it is not unlikely that in the immediate future there may be other seizures of power by the military, to either halt or moderate the pace of social change.

Nasserism

What will be the next step in Latin America's political evolution? As the social boiler continues to build up pressure and the military continues to sit on the lid, is a mass explosion and destruction of the armed forces inevitable? Such a violent consequence may indeed occur in some countries if the oligarchy and the armed forces—for different reasons, to be sure—continue their myopic resistance. After all, violent social upheavals have already occurred in Mexico, Bolivia, and Cuba. In each case, the explosion was precipitated by a military dictator ruling in league with a reactionary oligarchy. In still a fourth case, in Costa Rica in 1948, the armed forces were destroyed by an aroused civilian populace. The growing internecine warfare of the armed forces, of course, markedly increases their susceptibility to ultimate elimination by their own people.

If such social explosions should occur, what would be the outcome? Is it inevitable that authoritarian Communism would result, as in Cuba? The Mexican experience reveals little in the way of a historical lesson, for that upheaval took place before Communism had become a political force in the Western Hemisphere. However, in Costa Rica and Bolivia, the democratic elements that won power had little trouble in meeting the challenge of the Communists.

Though it is often asserted that a military power seizure is the only method that remains feasible in some countries to avert a Communist takeover, this assertion is not applicable in a single

Latin American country today. The appeal of Castro's brand of totalitarianism is not yet that great. Ironically, however, attempts by the armed forces to hold back the relentless pressures for social reform in order to prevent their countries from going "the Cuban way" ultimately increase the popular appeal of "the Cuban way." For when recourse to the ballot box, the law, and the constitution is cut off, the only remaining outlet for achieving social justice is violence. And in all the cases where the military have ousted popular governments during 1962, 1963, and 1964, civilian democratic elements not only have disputed their right to do so but also have become imbued with a spirit of revenge.

Yet it is too gloomy and unlikely a prospect that the *status quo* will remain unchanged until mass violence erupts everywhere. For although the demand for social change and reform is an irresistible force, the military organization is not an immovable object, despite appearances, in most Latin American countries today. The ruling generals and admirals are far more conservative on social problems than the colonels and commanders are, and the cadets and lieutenants, still relatively close in time to civilian life and its problems, are the most sensitive of all to the demands of society.

Another indication of the military's awakening social conscience is the internecine warfare among the various service branches, which became more serious during the early 1960's than at any previous time in Latin America's history. In the shooting, or near shooting, that has occurred thus far, armies have been the most responsive to social unrest, navies the blindest. Certainly this was the case in Brazil and Argentina. However, in Ecuador, it was the Air Force that preserved constitutionalism for two more years, in 1961, and in Venezuela it was the Navy that, in part, opted for extreme leftism.

What all this institutional rumbling presages is the gravitation of the armed forces toward a more sympathetic attitude toward the social problem. This seems inevitable as it becomes increasingly necessary for the military to consider the number of their countrymen they might have to shoot in order to maintain the present system.

But having rejected in so many countries the governing rights of civilian political organizations, the armed forces have themselves become saddled with the difficult tasks of conducting their nations down the tortuous pathways of sweeping structural reform in their societies, their economies, and perhaps their political systems, as well. Certainly there is more than an indication of the military's arrogating to itself the responsibility for some kind of reform in Brazil, El Salvador, Peru, and Ecuador today. These developments demonstrate clearly that the military in some countries is beginning to develop an ideology of its own.

There is also beginning to emerge now—and it will in all probability become much more prominent in the near future—that political phenomenon labeled "Nasserism." This merely means the assumption by the Latin American armed forces of the same kind of modernizing and reforming responsibilities that the military have assumed in the Near East. Nasserism is apt to develop in a variety of ways. It may occur in an evolutionary way as the present military hierarchy is replaced, in the normal course of retirements and promotions, by more responsible middle-rank officers. It may also occur, as in Argentina, by the defeat of reactionary service branches in internecine warfare. But a much more likely development is an institutional upheaval inside the armed forces. That is, junior- and middle-rank officers, apprehensive over the threat to the very existence of the armed-forces organization produced by the myopia of their commanders—and perhaps mixed with these motives will be individual desires for promotion and power—will attempt to overthrow the present military leadership.

Indications of the military's growing social consciousness are legion. The armed forces' pro-reform statements following the coups in Brazil, Peru, and Ecuador are significant in this context, as are the progressive stands of some segments of the armies of

Venezuela and Argentina today. The El Salvador experiment may be a forerunner of things to come. At the various Latin American war colleges, the middle-rank officers who are trained there receive courses in economics, sociology, political science, and national planning. Such schooling instills the trainees with confidence in themselves as future statesmen.

Nasserism, of course, is nothing new. At the end of World War II, for example, a national-reconstruction and social-reform mission was assumed by the armed forces in Argentina, Bolivia, Venezuela, Peru, Ecuador, Panama, El Salvador, and Colombia. Nearly all these experiments came to grief, however. The uniformed reformers left their nations, on the whole, in far worse condition than before. The near bankruptcy and social disintegration General Perón produced in Argentina, the tyranny and corruption perpetrated by the initially reform-minded regime of General Rojas Pinilla in Colombia, and the retrogressive and irresponsible dictatorship General Pérez Jiménez and his Army colleagues set up in Venezuela following their early cooperation with civilian political-reform movements are cases in point. Latin America has yet to produce a military statesman possessing the modernizing and reforming abilities of a Mustafa Kemal Ataturk, for example, or even of a Nasser. Paradoxically, Latin America's strongest political institution in terms of achieving power has thus far been the weakest in terms of exercising it effectively and responsibly.

What appears to be imminent today is a second wave of Nasserism, a renewed attempt by the military to govern, or at least to participate actively in the governing of, its countries in order to help solve their social problems. But, however well meaning the emerging new group of uniformed statesmen may be, their difficulties are going to be much greater than those of their predecessors. First of all, it is doubtful, despite recent advances in professional schooling, that military men have increased their governing capabilities sufficiently to manage nations in intense states of socio-political ferment. And even if their capabilities have improved, they will have to govern in an atmosphere heavily charged with civilian hostility. For it is not only the recently ousted labor-leftist political parties that are antagonistic; the center and right also deny the military's right to govern.

For all these reasons, the Middle Eastern *nasserista* plant is not apt to take root in Latin American soil, for not only do the military have far less prestige in Latin America than in Nasser's area, but the Latin American civilian political system today is much more broadly developed and sophisticated than that which exists in the Near East. Thus, any would-be neo-Nasserite experiment will soon founder on the rocks of civilian resistance. To maintain power, it will have to gravitate toward totalitarian techniques. This in turn will deter it from its reform objectives, and the net result will be an unprogressive dictatorship. More likely, would-be Nasserites, once in office, will foresee the insurmountable difficulties and hastily abandon their attempts to rule.

If the above analysis is valid, then it follows that of the three contesting political systems—Communism, democracy, and militarism—none is likely to dominate Latin America in the remainder of the 1960's. Communism has the least chance of all, since it is weak in the civilian sector, almost nonexistent in the military sector, and generally hated and detested by both these groups. What is likely is that political power will continue to oscillate among the military sector, the genuine democratic forces in the center and on the left, and the pseudo democrats on the right. The military will probably intervene again and again as new political crises, socially conditioned, confront the civilian authorities. Where the military decides against holding the reins of government itself, it will continue to try to decide who does, and until the armed forces themselves become more responsive to the social revolution, their choice will continue to be the pseudo democrats on the right. But this can only be temporary, for each counterrevolutionary government will in time be replaced, probably first by an interim Nasserite experiment, then by the irrepressible forces of social revolution. It is in this manner that the political pendulum is likely to oscillate in most Latin American countries—though violent upheavals are possible in some—as the social crisis gravitates toward partial resolution in the present decade.

9. Dilemma in Washington

Johnson and the Latin American Generals

Since his very first days in office, President Lyndon B. Johnson has had to deal with the problem of militarism in Latin America. In the last two months of the Kennedy Administration, the United States boycott—diplomatic, economic, and military—of the Dominican and Honduran regimes, as intended, seriously weakened the position of the military rulers in those two nations. But they soon came up with the magic formula for resisting demands to restore democracy and constitutionalism; it was the cry of Castro-Communism. Though Castro-Communism was never a serious problem when the democratic governments of Bosch and Villeda Morales were in power, the new military rulers repeatedly warned that Washington's ostracism of their regimes had given strength to subversive elements and that a Cuban-type upheaval was in store unless recognition and aid were granted. To this blackmail, the new Johnson Administration succumbed. On December 14, 1963, in exchange for assurances that some kind of elections would be held during 1965, the juntas in the Dominican Republic and Honduras were recognized. During January and February, 1964, the economic- and military-aid programs were resumed.

During March came further evidence that a basic policy shift was under way in Washington. On March 16, the third anniversary of the Alliance for Progress, President Johnson paid lip service to the United States' continued devotion to the principles of economic development, social justice, and human freedom for Latin America, but he made no mention of the principal internal impediments to freedom and social justice, namely, the military and the oligarchies. Instead, he mentioned that the principal threat to the Alliance was from Communism and in unequivocal terms pledged that "the full power of the United States is ready to assist any country where freedom is threatened by forces dictated from beyond the shores of the continent."*

But two days later, on March 18, at a meeting of United States ambassadors to Latin America, the new Assistant Secretary of State for Latin American Affairs, Thomas Mann, reportedly suggested that it was unwise for the United States to continue to become involved in internal threats to freedom in Latin America, since Kennedy's policies had demonstrated how fruitless it was for the United States to try to impose democracy upon Latin America. Mann urged that greater attention be paid to immediate national-security interests, such as protection of United States investments and resistance to Communism. He suggested a less passionate commitment to political freedom and social justice. The emerging "Mann doctrine" seemed to be that henceforth the United States would no longer oppose military coups or rightist dictatorships. Thus, the new, and much narrower, criteria for recognizing and supporting new governments in Latin America seemed to be anti-Communism and security for foreign investments. Eliminated were the Kennedy foreign-policy dimensions of human freedom and social justice. The United States seemed to be returning to the hard-nosed pragmatism that had characterized its foreign policy in Latin America between the end of World War II and 1960.

The military coup in Brazil put the new policies to their first test. The United States Government had long been concerned about President Goulart's softness on the Communist problem and his notoriously unsound economic policies. Hence it was quick to welcome a change. It side-stepped the recognition issue

* Speech at the Pan American Union.

by maintaining that since the presidency had been vacated and the constitutional successor had assumed office, no interruption of diplomatic ties was involved. Secretary of State Rusk saw the coup as a victory for democracy and constitutional government. The matter of how social justice would fare following the coup was ignored. If the Johnson Administration was concerned about the armed forces' subsequent assumption of control by installing their man in the Presidency, about their rendering Congress impotent and overriding the courts, about the widespread purges of democratically elected officials, about the press censorship and about the mass arrests, no public statement of its reservations was forthcoming from Washington.

Some Questions, Comments, and Suggestions

Despite the repeated frustration of Washington's efforts to control the political proclivities of the Latin American officer corps, the question arises as to whether it is in the best security interests of the United States to accept the resurgence of militarism in Latin America. Certainly it is clear that the greatest single impediment to democratic progress in Latin America today—though certainly not the only one—is the military. It is also true that the seven recent interventions have put a damper, at least temporarily, upon progress toward social reform. If it is in the best security interests of the United States that the evolutionary reform path be followed, then it should not be forgotten that every violent social upheaval that has shaken Latin America in the present century (in Mexico, Cuba, and Bolivia) has resulted primarily from the intransigence of military rulers in the face of popular pressures for change and reform.

Military rulers are very uncertain guarantors for United States security interests. No less than four armed-forces organizations (those of Mexico, Bolivia, Costa Rica, and Cuba) have been completely destroyed by their own people in the last half century, three of them in the past sixteen years. Was it not something very similar to the Mann doctrine—that is, acceptance of a military dictatorship which was anti-Communist and which protected United States investments—that played an important part in paving the way for the Castro regime of today?

The United States might well ask itself why the Communists have made Venezuelan democracy their number-one target in the early 1960's, why they were so intent upon provoking a rightist military coup. Also, does it not appear probable that the recent turn of events in Brazil will increase the Communists' long-term prospects in that country?

Has the Johnson Administration committed an error in apparently abandoning the pro-democracy dimension of United States Latin American policy that characterized the Kennedy years? What about the commitments to help promote democracy assumed by the United States in the Punta del Este charter? If it is proper or wise to remain indifferent to internal developments in Latin America so long as they do not disturb our day-to-day interests, what will be the consequence five to ten years from now? Are we not becoming associated with an alarmingly large number of counterrevolutionary governments in Latin America? Can we continue such association indefinitely and at the same time convince the people of Latin America that we are really for the principles of human freedom and social justice espoused under the Alliance for Progress? Will it not become increasingly impossible to get Congress to approve Alianza appropriations for regimes that are fundamentally opposed to Alianza principles?

Is it not high time for the United States to try to recapture her moral leadership in Latin America? Admittedly, nonrecognition has so far failed to prevent unrepresentative military regimes. But this is no reason to abandon all efforts to encourage democracy. The attempt to do so by eschewing all overt cooperation, including military and economic aid, with counterrevolutionary military regimes has not been given a full and fair trial as yet. Its trial in Peru, the Dominican Republic, and Honduras was abandoned too soon to have any effect. Carried to its conclusion, a nonrecognition policy may have several possible outcomes. The regime may be able to withstand United States pressures indefinitely; it may capitulate to United States demands to the extent of providing guarantees, not only that elections will be held soon, but also that genuine democracy will be restored; or it may be destroyed by its own people in a violent upheaval.

It is this latter eventuality that Washington fears most, but its fears that the Castro-Communists will capture any such revolution are exaggerated. Such apprehensions, or misapprehensions, reveal a lack of courage to face up to the social crisis. Inevitably in Latin America, and particularly in the most backward nations, where the military is unimaginative and unrealistically frightened of a Communist takeover, social change is bound to come through violence. The United States must be more willing to accept such a development and to do business with a government that emanates from a violent revolution. Such a policy worked in Bolivia; it can work elsewhere in Latin America. Ideally, the Alliance for Progress concept of peaceful, evolutionary change would be the most desirable; in historical practice, however, societies as backward as those in most of Latin America today have generally been changed only by violence.

There is another important consideration with respect to the whole reform problem that has apparently not been thought through yet to its logical conclusion. To be sure, the Communists are always going to associate themselves with, and try to capture control of, any movement for social change and reform. Broadly based popular groups intent upon breaking through the resistance of dictatorships and unrepresentative governments, and needing all the help they can get, will almost invariably have Communists in their movement—as Goulart did and as Rómulo Betancourt's forces did when they brought down the Pérez Jiménez dictatorship in Venezuela in 1958. But Communist association with a revolutionary movement need not mean Communist control of the triumphant revolution. What was the case in Cuba was not the result in Venezuela. And who can be sure what the ultimate outcome might have been in Brazil if Goulart had won out? By becoming panicked into cooperation with any force that raises the Castro-Communist bugaboo, we begin to commit ourselves to a policy of associating exclusively with counterrevolutionary governments. This is the image of the United States the Communists attempt to portray to the Latin American masses. We should do our utmost to avoid abetting them.

To the extent that counterrevolutionary militarism continues to be tacitly condoned, the Alliance for Progress degenerates into a purely technical program of financing economic- and social-development projects. If Washington is willing to accept authoritarian rule as the price of economic change and social reform, the major distinction between "the Cuban way" and "the American way" of social revolution disappears. For what has then happened to "freedom"? As Tad Szulc in his *Winds of Revolution** has so forcefully argued, the main weakness of the Alliance for Progress, the principal reason for its failure thus far, has been the lack of progress in the political sphere. Kennedy enunciated a policy of democratic idealism, but it was never strongly implemented in the field. Unless that political idealism is realistically oriented and strengthened, United States efforts in the social and economic realm will never succeed in capturing the hearts and minds of the Latin American people. It is only at the expense of its long-range world-wide image and security interests that the United States can accept military dictatorship or Nasserism as short cuts and forfeit the democratic means of attaining social and economic reform in Latin America.

With respect to military policies, the counterinsurgency program should be re-evaluated, and it must certainly be discontinued in those nations where the armed forces and the police apply counterinsurgency weapons and techniques in political situations that have nothing to do with Castro-Communism. Similarly, Washington should be extremely wary of the use made

* Frederick A. Praeger, 1963.

of its 7,000-man antiguerrilla force in the Canal Zone presumably on call for any Latin American government threatened by subversive disorders. To use this force at the behest of a nonrepresentative military regime could result in the gravest damage to the United States' popular image in Latin America. Finally, with respect to the policy of pumping large supplies of counterinsurgency weapons into Latin America, it should be remembered that the strategy of the guerrillas and the urban terrorists is to steal weapons rather than undertake the difficult and expensive task of clandestinely importing them. Thus, counterinsurgency preparations might also enhance the capabilities of the insurgents.

With respect to the conventional military policy of hemisphere defense, the time has finally come to rid the Latin American military organizations of the too-long-held delusion that they are preparing themselves for some glorious future war. Needlessly serving to perpetuate such a myth is the recently established Inter-American Defense College at Fort McNair, Washington, D.C., which trains about thirty-five Latin American officers every five months.* And certainly, inasmuch as the weapons granted for hemisphere defense are now used exclusively for interservice warfare and for overwhelming civilian governments, there is little or no justification for continuing the Military Defense Assistance agreements now in force with eleven Latin American nations, five of whose military organizations seized their governments during 1962 and 1963.

Not that such measures would be likely to promote disarmament, for little can really be done about the Latin American military's apparently insatiable demands for modern equipment. The reminder by Teodoro Moscoso, then Alliance for Progress Coordinator, at the Fourth Annual Conference of American Armies, in July, 1963, that one jet costs as much as 500 rural schools did nothing to deter the determination of Latin America's

---

* They are taught much about Communism here but little about democracy.

air forces to equip, or re-equip, themselves with squadrons of new jets. Similarly, the armies want modern tanks and artillery equipment, and the navies demand carriers, jet planes, submarines, and destroyers. The various services insist on this equipment to keep pace with each other as well as with their neighbors. What is more, Latin America's armed forces are sensitive to the ridicule heaped upon them by first-line military powers. They are determined to overcome the image of themselves as fourth-rate powers, which now prevails abroad and often at home, as well.

Various proposals, some of them rather bizarre, have been made for an inter-American armed force that might be used in defense against both Communism and militarism. One such proposal is for an OAS "fire brigade" to deal with such problems in individual nations. Similarly, the Senate Foreign Relations Committee has been trying for a number of years to get the Pentagon to encourage the formation of an OAS military force to perform peacekeeping functions in the hemisphere. Such proposals are almost certain to fail, as have nearly all those for collective action in the past, because of Latin America's insistence upon nonintervention.

When all is said and done, it becomes clear that militarism in Latin America is going to plague Washington for years to come. Until Latin America's military officers perceive alternate career opportunities, until they gain a better sense of institutional security, they are not going to sit by and see their power position undermined. They are a powerful political force that can neither be eliminated nor be easily controlled. They have to be accepted as a fact of Latin American political life and dealt with accordingly. The political approach to the military problem, that is, the encouragement of Nasserism, is fraught with dangers and disadvantages to American security. The most fruitful policy, despite the recent setbacks, is to continue the efforts to make the Latin American military good soldiers, to try to convince them that they should eschew politics completely, that they must learn to become the tools rather than the masters of the state, that they must devote themselves exclusively to legitimate military functions. The armed forces must be made to understand that their survival demands greater acceptance of evolutionary change today in order to avoid violent revolution tomorrow. In this manner, the democratic ideal will have its best opportunity for eventual realization in Latin America.

Bibliography

ADAMS, RICHARD N. (ed.). *Social Change in Latin America Today*. New York: Harper & Bros., 1960.

ALBA, VÍCTOR. *El Militarismo*. Mexico City: Editorial Cultura, 1960.

ALEXANDER, ROBERT. *Communism in Latin America*. New Brunswick, N.J.: Rutgers University Press, 1957.

———. *Today's Latin America*. New York: Doubleday & Co., 1962.

ALMOND, GABRIEL, and COLEMAN, JAMES S. *The Politics of the Developing Areas*. Princeton, N.J.: Princeton University Press, 1960.

ANDRZEJEWSKI, STANISLAW. *Military Organization and Society*. London: Routledge and Kegan Paul, 1954.

ARCINIEGAS, GERMÁN. *The State of Latin America*. New York: Alfred A. Knopf, 1952; London: Cassell & Co., 1953.

BARROSO, GUSTAVO. *Historia Militar do Brasil*. São Paulo: Editora Nacional, 1935.

BAZÁN PÉREZ, JUAN. *El Ejército en la Constitución y en la Política*. Mexico City, 1952.

CHRISTENSEN, ASHER N. *The Evolution of Latin American Governments*. New York: Henry Holt, 1951.

DAVIS, HAROLD E. (ed.). *Government and Politics in Latin America*. New York: The Ronald Press, 1958.

DREIER, JOHN C. *The Organization of American States and the Hemisphere Crisis*. New York: Harper & Row, 1962.

ESPAILLAT, ARTURO. *Trujillo: The Last Caesar*. Chicago: Henry Regnery Co., 1963.

FERGUSON, J. HALCRO. *The Revolutions of Latin America*. London: Thames and Hudson, 1963.

FINER, S. E. *The Man on Horseback*. London: Pall Mall Press, 1960; New York: Frederick A. Praeger, 1962.

FLUHARTY, VERNON L. *Dance of the Millions: Military Rule and the Social Revolution in Colombia, 1930–1956*. Pittsburgh, Pa.: University of Pittsburgh Press, 1957.

FREYRE, GILBERTO. *Nação e Exército*. Rio de Janeiro: J. Olympio, 1949.

FURNISS, EDGAR S., JR. *American Military Policy*. New York: Rinehart & Co., 1957.

GARCÍA LUPO, ROGELIO. *La Rebelión de los Generales*. Buenos Aires: Proceso, 1962.

HUNTINGTON, SAMUEL P. *The Soldier and the State: The Theory and Politics of Civil-Military Relations*. Cambridge, Mass.: Harvard University Press, 1957.

JANE, CECIL. *Liberty and Despotism in Latin America*. Oxford: The Clarendon Press, 1929.

JANOWITZ, MORRIS. *The Military in the Political Development of New Nations*. Chicago: The University of Chicago Press, 1964.

————. *The Professional Soldier*. Glencoe, Ill.: The Free Press of Glencoe, 1960.

JOHNSON, JOHN J. *The Military and Society in Latin America*. Stanford, Calif.: Stanford University Press, 1964.

————. (ed.). *The Role of the Military in Underdeveloped Countries*. Princeton, N.J.: Princeton University Press, 1962.

KAUTSKY, JOHN (ed.). *Political Change in Underdeveloped Countries*. New York: John Wiley & Sons, 1962.

LIEUWEN, EDWIN. *Arms and Politics in Latin America*. Rev. ed. New York: Frederick A. Praeger, 1961.

————. *Venezuela*. London and New York: Oxford University Press, 1961.

MADARIAGA, SALVADOR DE. *Latin America Between the Eagle and the Bear*. New York: Frederick A. Praeger; London: Hollis & Carter, 1962.

MANCERA GALLETI, ANGEL. *Civilismo y Militarismo*. Caracas, 1960.

MATTHEWS, HERBERT L. (ed.). *The United States and Latin America*. New York: American Assembly, 1959.

MECHAM, J. LLOYD. *The United States and Inter-American Security, 1889–1960*. Austin, Tex.: University of Texas Press, 1961.

MILLIKAN, MAX F., and BLACKMER, DONALD (eds.). *The Emerging Nations*. Boston: Little, Brown, 1961; London and Bombay: Asia Publishing House, 1962.

NAVARRO, PEDRO JUAN. *Dictadores de América*. Bogotá: Mundoaldía, 1936.

NEEDLER, MARTIN. *Latin American Politics in Perspective*. Princeton, N.J.: D. Van Nostrand Co., 1963.

POWELSON, JOHN P. *Latin America: Today's Economic and Social Revolution*. New York: McGraw-Hill, 1964.

RAMOS, JORGE ABELARDO. *Historia Política del Ejército Argentina*. Buenos Aires: Pena Lillo, 1959.

SAPIN, BURTON M., and SNYDER, RICHARD C. *The Role of the Military in American Foreign Policy.* New York: Doubleday & Co., 1954.

SCHMITT, KARL M., and BURKS, DAVID D. *Evolution or Chaos: Dynamics of Latin American Politics.* New York: Frederick A. Praeger, 1963; London: Pall Mall Press, 1964.

SCHNEIDER, RONALD M. *Communism in Guatemala, 1944–1954.* New York: Frederick A. Praeger, 1958.

SZULC, TAD. *Twilight of the Tyrants.* New York: Henry Holt, 1959.

————. *The Winds of Revolution.* New York: Frederick A. Praeger, 1963.

TANNENBAUM, FRANK. *Ten Keys to Latin America.* New York: Alfred A. Knopf, 1963.

VAGTS, ALFRED. *Defense and Diplomacy.* New York: King's Crown Press, 1956.

————. *History of Militarism.* New York: W. W. Norton & Co., 1937; London: Allen & Unwin, 1938.

VILLANUEVA, VÍCTOR. *Militarismo en el Perú.* Lima: Empress Gráfica T. Schench, 1962.

Index

Acción Democrática party of Venezuela, 91

Acosta Velasco, Jaime, 49

Agrarian reform, 4, 100, 102; in Peru, 35; in Guatemala, 40; in Ecuador, 47, 51, 52; in Honduras, 66; in Brazil, 75, 77, 83; in Venezuela, 86; in El Salvador, 94

Alessandri, Arturo, 46

Alliance for Progress, 102, 115, 146; Kennedy proposes, 3; program of, 3, 4; Charter, 4, 145; resurgence of militarism setback for, 6, 110; financial assistance to Frondizi under, 12; Ecuador's social reforms under, 51; approves Villeda Morales' program for Honduras, 66; economic aid to Peru cut by, 116

Alsina, Cayo Antonio, 17, 18, 21

Alsogaray, Alvaro, 12

Anselmo, José, 80

Anti-*peronistas,* 10, 13, 14, 16, 23

AP (Popular Action Party of Peru), 26–27

APRA (American Revolutionary Popular Alliance of Peru), 28, 29, 107; dominant party, 26, 27; controls organized labor, 30, 100; competition with military, 31, 35; social-reform program, 33; alliance with oligarchy, 34

Aramburu, Pedro, 11–12, 13, 14, 17

Arana, Francisco Javier, 39, 41, 42

Arbenz, Jacobo, 38, 40, 41, 42

Arévalo, Juan, 39–40, 42, 107, 117

Argentina, 11, 12; military intervention in, 4, 7, 106, 107, 130; 1962

elections, 4, 10; military coup of 1962, 4–5, 17–22, 115–16; Army, 14, 16, 17, 18, 19–20, 23; Navy, 15, 16, 19, 21–22; Air Force, 17, 21, 22, 23; armed forces, decision-making process of, 17; labor-leftist forces in, 22–24

Armed forces: political role of, 3–8, 95–98, 130–31; role in social reform, 5–9, 34, 101, 130–31, 135, 139; and democracy, 7, 130–35; extramilitary functions, 95–96; corporate self-interest, 106–7; as segment of corrupt body politic, 113; internecine warfare in, 137

Arosemena, Julio Carlos, 5n., 45–49, 105, 118, 123

Arraes, Miguel, 70, 83

Arroyo del Río, Carlos, 52

Balaguer, Joaquín, 56, 57, 58

Balbín, Ricardo, 12

Barrios, Justo Rufino, 40

Barros, Adhemar de, 69, 79

Batista, Fulgencio, 4, 101, 124

Belaúnde Terry, Fernando, 26, 27, 29, 32, 36; assigns social-reconstruction role to armed services, 35, 106, 132

Beltrán, Pedro, 34

Benavides, Oscar, 28

Betancourt, Rómulo, 56; serves out constitutional term, 86, 132; achievements, 86; sympathetic to armed forces, 87–88; military rebellions against, 89; orders arrest of leftist extremists, 90; anti-Communist, 106

Bevilaqua, Pery Constant, 74n.

Birnbaum, Maurice, 45, 118
Bolívar, Simón, quoted, 28
Bolivia: destroys Army, 8, 131, 144; attitude toward Cuba, 126n.; apolitical posture of armed forces, 130
Borgas, Sílvio, 80
Bosch, Juan: deposed, 5, 53, 60–62, 127; charged with corruption, 53–54; refuses to outlaw Communism, 54, 105, 106; anti-Communist record, 54, 64, 106; reform policies and rightist criticism of, 55, 58–61; PRD support of, 57, 61, 62, 63; U.S. attitude toward, 54, 118
Brazil: military rule in, 5, 7, 106; social crisis, 70–71, 75, 80; disenfranchisement of illiterates, 71, 77; economic development under Kubitschek, 72; constitutional crisis of 1961, 73–75; Army-Navy rivalry, 75; political independence of Air Force, 75–76; National Peasant Confederation, 77–78; Goulart consolidates power, 76–78; opposition to Goulart, 78–80; armed-forces rebellion, 80–81; Institutional Act, 82, 83; responsibility of military leaders, 83–84, 138; comparison with Argentine military intervention, 84–85, 101, 130
Briceño Linares, Antonio, 89, 90
Brizola, Leonel, 75, 78, 83
Burrows, Charles, 119
Bustamante, José Luis, 29, 33

Cabrera Sevilla, Luis, 50
Carlson, Frank, 128
Caro, Luis, 20
Carrera, Rafael, 40
Carreras, Mariano Bartolomé, 18
Castelo Branco, Humberto, 82, 83–85
Castillo Armas, Carlos, 4, 38, 41
Castro, Fidel, 50, 122, 142; attraction for masses, 6, 54, 101, 102, 137; destroys Batista's armed forces, 101, 124; reorganizes military, 132–33; threat to Ecuador, 50; messianic mission of, 134
Castro, Raúl, 132
Castro Jijón, Ramón, 50

Chile, 6; apolitical posture of armed forces, 8, 131; attitude toward Cuba, 126n.
China, 133
Colombia, 6; apolitical posture of armed forces, 8, 131
Communism, 148n.; danger of, 6, 8; surveillance by U.S., 54, 105; military fear of, 105–6
Costa Rica, 121; destroys regular Army, 8, 131, 136, 144
Counterinsurgency, 6, 147–48
Cuba, 6, 46; fall of Batista, 4, 101, 124; U.S. relations with, 121–23; Eisenhower's attitude toward, 122; authoritarian Communism in, 132
Cunha Rodríguez, Paulo María da, 80

Dantas, Jair, 70
Denys, Odílio, 73, 74
Dominican Republic, 7, 8; assassination of Trujillo, 4, 56, 115; military intervention in, 5, 53, 106, 130; military coup deposes Bosch, 53, 59–61, 62, 127; U.S. relations with, 54, 62, 118–19, 127, 142; conservative civilian junta, 53, 62, 118–19; political stability under Trujillo, 55; military establishment under Trujillo, 55–56; economic progress, 56; Catholic Church in, 56–58, 59; and OAS, 56, 57, 142; Council of State, 57, 59; Air Force, 62–63; Navy, 63
Duvalier, François, 60–61, 130n.

Ecuador: military intervention in, 5, 45, 48–49, 51–52, 106, 107, 130; constitutional government in, 45; military coup in 1963, 45 ff.; pro-Castro guerrillas in, 46–47; pro-Communist conspiracy in Army, 47; Army engineers and Air Force rebel, 48, 137; social reform, 51; U.S. confidence in, 51; military and reform, 138
Eisenhower, Dwight D., Administration of, 114, 122
El Salvador, 4, 6, 7; society of, 91–93; domination by armed forces, 91–92; reform junta, 93, 132; accomplish-

ments of Rivera, 94; promises of elections and constitutional government, 114; military and reform, 138
Estrado Cabrera, Rafael, 40

FALN (Armed Forces of National Liberation of Venezuela), 90
FAP (Popular Action Front of Chile), 131
Fiallo, Viriato Alberto, 57
Freile Posso, Guillermo, 50
Frondizi, Arturo: deposed, 5, 114; reasons for fall, 10–13; key role of Navy in downfall, 16; armed forces united against, 17; charged with Communism, 105
Furtado, Celso, 83

Gándara Enríquez, Marcos, 50
Gorilas, 14, 16–17, 19, 21, 22
Goulart, João: revolt against, 5, 69; flees to Brasília, 70; Third Army loyal to, 70, 73–74; exiled, 70; unacceptable to officers of armed forces, 72, 73; Congress antagonistic to, 74–78 passim; economic chaos under, 76–77, 81; reform efforts, 77–78, 79; Communist support of, 78, 105, 143; Catholic Church opposes, 78-79; Army-Navy ultimatum, 80-81; pro-Cuban policy, 123; U.S. concern over economic policies, 143
Grantham, Carlos, 36
Green Dragon Lodge (Argentina), 13–14, 17
Gruening, Ernest, 128
Grum Moss, Gabriel, 73, 74
Guatemala: assassination of Armas, 4; military intervention in, 5, 7, 106; training site for Cuban exiles, 37; political stability under military dictatorships, 40, 103, 107; 1963 Army coup, 42–43, 117; U.S. relations with, 117–18
Guido, José María, 18, 19, 20, 21, 22, 115; puppet of military, 19, 115–16

Haiti, 4, 6, 8
Hammer and Piston Lodge (Argentina), 14

Haya de la Torre, Víctor Raúl, 26, 27, 28, 29, 30, 32, 106, 116
Heck, Sílvio, 73, 74
Honduras, 103, 107; military intervention in, 5, 106, 130; 1963 military coup, 5, 7, 63, 65–66; future role of military, 8; social structure of, 64; Civil Guard, 66, 68; Army police power, 68; U.S. relations with, 68, 119, 120, 142
Humphrey, Hubert H., 116

Illía, Arturo, 22
Inter-American Treaty of Reciprocal Assistance (Rio Pact), 96, 122

Johnson, Lyndon B., 54; policy toward Latin American military, 6, 142–43
Julião, Francisco, 83
Jurema, Abelardo, 83

Kennedy, John F., 116, 117, 118, 119; proposes Alliance for Progress, 3, 115; policy toward Latin American military, 6, 114–15; and counterinsurgency program, 6, 124–27 passim; speech in Miami, 120; and Cuban question, 121 ff.; criticism of policies, 128–29
Kingman Riofrío, Nicolás, 46
Kruel, Amaury, 69, 70
Kubitschek, Juscelino, 72, 83

Lacerda, Carlos, 70, 79
Larrazábal, Carlos, 88
Larrazábal, Wolfgang, 87, 88
Legalistas, 19–20, 24
Lemus, José María, 4, 92
Leoni, Raúl, 91
Liberal Party of Honduras, 65, 66, 67
Lindley López, Nicolás, 30, 31
Loeb, James, 116
Lonardi, Eduardo, 13, 16, 17
López, Oswaldo, 63–64, 65, 67, 68, 119, 120
Lott, Henrique Teixeira, 72, 73
Loza, Juan Bautista, 18, 19
Lozano, Julio, 65
Luna, Atila, 60
Luna, Julio, 36

MAAG (Military Advisory Assistance Group of the United States), 118, 119

McLaughlin, Eduardo, 21

Magalhaes Pinto, José, 69

Magloire, Paul, 4

Mann, Thomas C., 143; "Mann doctrine," 143–45

Martejena, Pío, 14

Martin, John B., 118

Mazzilli, Ranieri, 70, 75

Mexico, 8, 131; attitude toward Cuba, 101, 126n.

Militarism, 3, 4, 5, 8, 91, 92; and Alliance for Progress, 6, 145, 147, 148–49; analysis of, 7; as political force, 135; resurgence of, 144 ff.

Military intervention: coups depose constitutional presidents: in Argentina, 5, 84–88, 100, 101; in Peru, 5, 7, 106, 107, 130; in Guatemala, 5, 7, 100, 106; in Ecuador, 5, 45, 48–49, 51–52, 100, 106, 107, 130; in Dominican Republic, 5, 53, 106, 130; in Honduras, 5, 100, 106, 130; decision-making power: in Argentina, 17–25 passim; in Peru, 25–26, 28, 29–30, 32, 106; in Brazil, 69–70, 84–85, 101; in Venezuela, 87, 100; in El Salvador, 92, 100; preventive coups, 102–7; and political instability, 102–3; decision to intervene, 103, 106, 107, 108; aftermath, 108–9; political and social consequences, 109–10, 129; civilian view of, 111–12; Kennedy's disapproval of, 112; U.S. view of, 117

Morse, Wayne, 128

Moscoso, Teodoro, 148

Mourão, Olímpio, 69

Nasserism, 136–41

Nationalist Party of Honduras, 64–65, 66, 67, 106

Neomilitarism, 9

Nicaragua, 4, 6, 8

Nixon, Richard M., 114n.

OAS (Organization of American States), 44n., 121; expels Cuba, 46, 48; expels Dominican Republic, 56, 57; approves blockade of Cuba, 123; imposes sanctions against Cuba, 126; peacekeeping role of, 96, 149

Odría, Manuel, 4, 7, 26; unacceptable to military, 27, 33, 35; military dictatorship of, 29, 33; social-reform program of, 33–35

Onganía, Juan, 14, 20

Orthodox Republican Party of Honduras, 66

Panama, 4, 8, 131

Paraguay, 4, 6, 8

PCN (National Conciliation Party of El Salvador), 93

Penas, Augustín A., 17

Peralta Azurdia, Enrique, 37, 42, 43, 44, 68

Pérez Godoy, Manuel, 26, 30, 31

Pérez Jiménez, Marcos, 4; military dictatorship of, 86–87, 88, 91, 139; Air Force and Navy revolt against, 87; coups attempted by associates, 89

Perón, Juan, 10; deposed, 4; Frondizi's deal with peronistas, 12; Navy opposes, 15–16; returns and consolidates power, 15, 100; Air Force and, 16, 23

Peronista Front (peronistas), 19, 107; 1962 election, 4, 10, 13; armed forces' reaction to 1962 election, 10, 23; outlawed in 1958, 12; Aramburu purges, 13; against gorilas, 14; Guido's compromise, 18; alliance with UCRI, 21, 22; and labor-left, 23, 24; and Nasserism, 24, 25

Peru: fall of Odría, 4, 7; military intervention in, 5, 26, 28, 107; junta rule, 5, 26–27, 30–32, 35; domination by military and oligarchy, 27–28; oligarchy, 28, 30, 32–33, 34; apristas, 28, 29, 107; military dictatorship under Odría, 33–34; Center for Advanced Military Studies, 34–35; military and reform, 32, 36, 138; U.S. relations with, 116–17

Peruvian Democratic Party, 29

Poggi, Raúl A., 14, 17–18

Ponce, Camilo, 49
Popular Socialist Party of Dominican Republic, 54
Popular Union of Argentina, 22
Portillo, Aníbal, 92
Prado, Manuel, 25–26, 28–29, 30, 127
Prestes, Luiz Carlos, 78, 83
PRD (Dominican Revolutionary Party), 57, 61, 62
PTB (General Confederation of Labor of Brazil), 78, 100
Punta del Este meetings: 1961, 4; 1962, 46, 122–23

Quadros, Jânio, 72–73, 77, 83

Raimundes, Manuel, 13–14
Rauch, Enrique, 18, 19
Rio Pact, see Inter-American Treaty of Reciprocal Assistance
Ríos, Sosa, 88
Rivera, Julio, 92–94
Rodas Alvarado, Modesto, 63, 66, 107
Rodríguez Echevarría, Pedro, 57
Rojas, Isaac, 15
Rojas Pinilla, Gustavo, 4, 139
Rojas Silveyra, Jorge, 18
Rosas, Carlos, 24
Rubottom, Roy R., 23n.
Rusk, Dean, 119, 144

Sánchez Cerro, Luis, 28
Señorans, Eduardo, 19
Somoza, Anastasio, 4
Stroessner, Alfredo, 4
Szulc, Tad, 147

Taxation, 4; revision urged: in Peru, 35; in Ecuador, 47, 51, 52; in Honduras, 66; in Brazil, 79; in Venezuela, 86; in El Salvador, 93, 94; threatens social groups, 102
Texeira, Florencio, 36
Toledo, Camilo Gallegos, 48
Toranzo Montero, Carlos, 14, 19
Toranzo Montero, Federico, 19, 20, 21
Torres Matos, Francisco, 30
Trujillo, Rafael Leónidas: assassinated, 4, 56, 115; anniversary of massacres, 29; political stability under, 55; U.S. Marines back, 55; bilks nation, 55–56; properties nationalized, 57

Ubico, Jorge, 37, 40
UCN (National Civil Union of the Dominican Republic), 57–58
UCRI (Intransigent Radical Civic Union of Argentina), 11, 12, 24, 31
UCRP (Popular Radical Civic Union of Argentina), 11, 12, 22, 24
Union of Soviet Socialist Republics, 113–34
United States: policy toward military, 3, 6; policy changed by Kennedy, 6, 114; foreign-policy objectives, 9; civic-action programs, 6; emergency assistance to Frondizi, 12; protests military coup in Peru, 30, 116; influence of, 34; and Ecuador, 51; attitude toward Bosch, 54, 118; pressure on Dominican junta, 62, 115, 118–19; suspends diplomatic relations with Honduras, 68, 119, 120; recognizes new Honduras government, 68; and anti-Communism, 105; and military coup in Argentina, 115; recognizes Peru, 116; restores aid to Peru, 117; and military coup in Guatemala, 117–18; sells arms to Latin America, 122
UNO (Odriísta National Union of Peru), 26–27
Urrutia, Gonzalo Almeida, 46
Uruguay, 8, 130–31; attitude toward Cuba, 101, 126n.

Varea Donosa, Reynaldo, 45, 49
Vargas, Getúlio, 72, 77, 81, 100
Vargas Prada, Pedro, 30n.
Velasco Ibarra, José María, 47–48, 49, 52–54, 107
Venezuela, 121; fall of Pérez Jiménez, 4; prospect of further coups, 6; role of armed forces, 7; economic development and social changes, 86; Betancourt and Castro-Communist strategy, 88, 89–90; leftist military rebels, 89; and OAS, 121, 126; future of democracy, 132

Villeda Morales, Ramón, 5, 63, 66, 111; war with Communists, 64; courts armed forces, 65; accused of Communist sympathies, 105; ouster, 63, 68

Viñas Román, Víctor Elby, 53, 60

Wessin y Wessin, Elías, 59–60

Ydígoras Fuentes, Manuel, 5, 37; charged with pro-Communism, 37, 105; aid to Cuban exiles, 37; Army grievances against, 37–38; Air Force attacks, 39; Army coup against, 39, 42; agrarian and tax reforms of, 41, 43–44; terrorism during Administration, 41–42; inefficiency of, 42